SCIENCE and SPIRITUALITY

Carmen D'Alessio

BALBOA.
PRESS

A DIVISION OF HAY HOUSE

Balboa Press books may be ordered through booksellers or by contacting:

Balboa Press
A Division of Hay House
1663 Liberty Drive
Bloomington, IN 47403
www.balboapress.com
1 (877) 407-4847

Because of the dynamic nature of the Internet, any web addresses or links contained in this book may have changed since publication and may no longer be valid. The views expressed in this work are solely those of the author and do not necessarily reflect the views of the publisher, and the publisher hereby disclaims any responsibility for them.

The author of this book does not dispense medical advice or prescribe the use of any technique as a form of treatment for physical, emotional, or medical problems without the advice of a physician, either directly or indirectly. The intent of the author is only to offer information of a general nature to help you in your quest for emotional and spiritual well-being. In the event you use any of the information in this book for yourself, which is your constitutional right, the author and the publisher assume no responsibility for your actions.

Any people depicted in stock imagery provided by Thinkstock are models, and such images are being used for illustrative purposes only. Certain stock imagery © Thinkstock.

Print information available on the last page.

ISBN: 978-1-5043-3817-2 (sc)
ISBN: 978-1-5043-3819-6 (hc)
ISBN: 978-1-5043-3818-9 (e)

Library of Congress Control Number: 2015912773

Balboa Press rev. date: 9/17/2015

FOREWORD

As bilinguals of dual Nationality, (we grew up in the UK of Italian parents who immigrated in 1950), I believe the daily interface between these two similar yet different cultures enriches and broadens one's mind and character, but also brings to naturally acquiring an unusually strong sensitivity that leaves you open to embracing the differences of others without prejudice and, moreover, with a welcoming smile.

Such is the case of the author of this book, my sister Carmen D'Alessio, who although in her sixties is still incredibly young at heart, in spirit and mind. With her naturally strong sense of curiosity and her yearning for knowledge, in recent years Carmen has felt an ever impelling urge to acquire a deeper understanding of our Human Universe.

An inspiring and absorbing book that spans form Western to Eastern ways of life, mingling spirituality and science with a hint of sociology, but above all providing clues of wisdom that may help us enrich the way we live our lives.

Brought up a Catholic, whilst not abandoning this religious belief, after her divorce she felt the need to pursue other practices to find the spirituality she needed and desired. Mingled with health problems that have ailed her along the way and disillusioned by the conventional expectations both spiritually and health wise, Carmen, with her generous and open heart as always and with an open mind, approached and experienced other religious beliefs in a search for a greater spiritual awareness. At the same time she also approached and experimented alternative medical fields that could aid the healing process.

A quest for peace of spirit, mind, and body.

Through a long and tortuous path, full of many and unusual experiences and with great commitment on her part, Carmen endeavored, and endeavors still, to find her own personal "truth," but one which in the end also brings a new light to all healing processes.

The book develops in three main parts, or if you like three main themes that, although seemingly different are inevitably intertwined. The opening introduces a Professor of Medicine and Scientist, Professor Corbucci from Viterbo, Italy, who has developed a futuristic instrument for the cure of the knee and many other problems connected to the spine. Professor Corbucci uses a scientific approach to spiritual beliefs in healing. We all know that everything is made of energy, Einstein's theory of relativity proved that everything, both those things we don't see and those we do see are all energy, even "mass" is energy. The ancient Chinese mapped out the "meridians'" within our body and all Eastern cultures are fully aware of the seven main energy points, the "Chakras."

The experience Carmen had with Prof. Corbucci has allowed her to develop an inspiring link between scientific and spiritual theories.

This brings us to the second part of the book, linking the authors search for spiritual awareness and energy healing, and she explains how she always felt impelled to learn more, thus how she became a Master in the ancient "cosmic energy" technique mostly referred to as "*Reiki*." Carmen recalls her own personal experiences along the arduous paths that have brought her to this practice and inspired her to write this book. Among her many travels she recounts some of the more important experiences encountered spanning from Africa, to

South and North India and to Tibet. An exciting insight into cultures that are extremely different from one another but that, ultimately, all have one common denominator, humbleness, spiritual awareness, humanity.

The third section, a spontaneous result of her search into the spiritual, inevitably delves into the intriguing world of the paranormal, an "energy" that we cannot see and it addresses the belief, deemed to be a fact by many Eastern cultures, that of re-incarnation. The Spirit is therefore considered to be an eternal energy that may regenerate itself and be reborn after death to follow the destiny of its new life, again and again. Think of those people who know another language without ever having studied it, were they in another nation in a past life? And what of those strong feelings of *Deja vous*, a premonition or memories from a past life? Here Carmen recalls how she re-lived her own past lives, memories, sensations and feelings that came to the surface during various spiritual healing sessions.

These Three themes are all inevitably connected and intermingle to give a global approach to what we may experience in life. Carmen narrates these topics and much more in a novelistic style that is captivating and enriching. Throughout the book you will read many impressive stories that the author has to tell, fruit of her own fascinating experiences, that will probably leave you in awe! These include encountering with meaningful world personalities such as the Dalai Lama, and the Indian spiritual guide Sai-Baba.

Carmen wishes wholeheartedly to share her many exceptional experiences, also in the hope that they may one day be beneficial to others too. To read this book, is to discover that not all is lost, there is a light at the end of the tunnel, if only we would open our eyes and our hearts and let the light shine in.

Rosa D'Alessio

Dedicated to my children, Sonia and Piero who are the best part of me, and to my wonderful grandchildren, Aurora, Alessandro and Gabriel who every day are a source of wonder and enrichment, together with my two acquired grandchildren.

Dedicated to my second husband Edoardo, who, although unaware, with love and dedication accompanies me on this spiritual path allowing me to make constant progress.

INTRODUCTION

This text is dedicated to all those who are open enough to accept that there may be other methods, beyond those known, to heal our bodies. A method of the future, which has come to us in advance, as a great gift. This book is dedicated to all people who work with the energies, and especially to all the Reiki Masters, second and first level Reiki practitioners, Yoga Teachers as well as all those millions of people who understand something or have anything to do with chakras.

I wish to share my astonishment and joy at discovering the scientific explanations given by an Italian Scientist to so many aspects of my spiritual path.

I hope with all my heart that our future generations can benefit from this technique, this knowledge, this non invasive science, to cure their body of the many health problems un-suspectedly connected to the spine. May the illuminating insight of a great mind be of benefit to all mankind. May this technique of the far future, together with Humanistic Reiki of the distant past, become the most commonly used methods for Human Beings to maintain their health.

This is especially dedicated to all those who are in search …

WHO IS MASSIMO CORBUCCI

Massimo Corbucci was born in Viterbo in 1954 and is a physician and surgeon as well as an esteemed Scientist. He collaborated with the GSI (Scientific Institution) in Darmstadt, Germany, for the 113th Atom issue, indicating a proven limit derived from his Scientific studies of 112 Atoms only, the 113th does not exist! As a Scientist, he had the audacity to suggest to the greatest authority of the Nuclear Physics in the World, the CERN in Geneva, in the person of the Director Maiani, to turn off everything, to switch off all the machinery, with regards to the Higg's Boson, in order not to experience an inglorious failure, and until today, despite the declarations and the efforts of CERN, the facts prove him right.

Director of the department of Legal Medicine of the ASL 04 (National Health Service) of Viterbo in Italy; Doctor and Nuclear Physicist, he graduated in medicine and surgery at the "Sapienza" University of Rome in 1984, with a Thesis on Electro- Physiology characteristics, Vettor-cardiografic syndrome Wolff-Parkinson-White. Corbucci has developed a revolutionary method of minimally invasive neuron microsurgery (Method DMC), which works on the principle of neuron-electronic-based Theory of Physics known as "Everything" or "Totalness" This method allows very important clinical diagnosis, which in turn allows to intervene successfully by treating problems un-curable in the present "state of the art" in medicine and surgery. Corbucci is the physicist who discovered the QMV (QuanticMechanicalVoid). He is editor of the journal "Science and Knowledge".

The books he has written include: *What are they and how many are the Chemical Elements,* World Scientific Publishing, September 2008; *Discovering the "God particle,"* Macro Remainders, January 2009; *The Physics of Intention,* Submerged Lands, April 2010; *Two Particles are Missing,* Macro Edizioni, October 2012. *The Physics of Chance* – I Libri del Casato Editors, November 2013.

CHAPTER 1

It's true that we must be careful what we ask (of the universe, archangels, etc.) because we can receive an answer!

I absolutely did not want to have knee surgery because I have varicose veins. Just as I was trying to make a decision regarding operating on my knee, my sister-in-law, Marika, who lives in New York, told me of the possibility that I could host the archangels for five days. During this time I prayed several times to receive guidance on what to do in order to avoid the operation. Late at night following one of these moments, I went to the computer because I was thinking about going to see what Dr. Hammer (a German alternative doctor) suggested regarding severe knee impediment.

I typed into Google "cure bad knee pains," and in the first line of the response I saw a noninvasive technique that intrigued me a lot, so I entered the site for more information. I found a surgeon who was also a nuclear scientist and physicist. He was well-known and highly respected in the scientific world. Twenty-five years earlier he had an illuminating insight and built an electronic computerized device for the treatment of the spinal column and therefore also severe knee pains, as well as many other pathologies.

I felt a strong urge to try this new "alternative and different" technique and found the doctor's telephone number on the site. A few explanations over the phone the next day definitely made my mind up. I called his secretary right away and fixed a time for the first treatments.

The meeting with this doctor completely turned me upside down. He opened new horizons to me, and my consciousness opened wide regarding various issues. I recovered ten years of health. I no longer have cervical pains, the cause of which were never identified by anyone, my veins are no longer swollen, and the size of my knees has been reduced by more than ten centimeters and they no longer hurt me! But let's take one step at a time.

I approach this book with great humility and simple language, as I am incompetent in the scientific field since my training in life is totally different. It is commercial for the most part and definitely more spiritual. Also because I am a humanistic Reiki master, l want to bring to the attention of all those who are ready to receive it this new and futuristic approach to a problem of physical pain that usually is solved with surgery.

Prof. Massimo Corbucci is a scientist who is deeply and sincerely dedicated to the service and welfare of mankind. He is a great mind who really understands the human body and looks at it as a whole, or as they say in the language of New Age, in a holistic manner.

In fact Plato said, "It is useless to try and cure one part of the body without looking at the wholeness, likewise it is useless to cure the body forgetting the Spirit. Therefore if you wish for the head and the body to be in good health, you must start by curing the mind. This comes first because it is in this that the error of our times resides."

When he was still very young, Prof. Corbucci sensed with incredible brilliance that the spine is just as important (and somewhat more) as the brain or head. He found the strength to pursue this brilliant idea until he conceived, developed, created, and patented an electronic device connected to multiple computers. Through electrical impulses the apparatus is able to investigate and identify in the spine exactly which of the thousands of neurons do not respond correctly, resulting in pain.

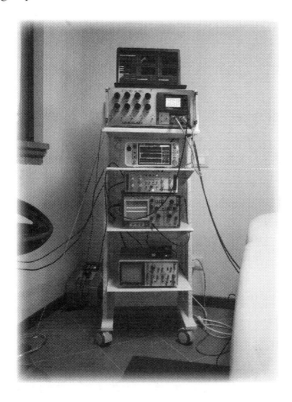

The machine signals with high precision any anomaly in the functionality of the neurons of the column. By leveraging his skills and knowledge as a nuclear physicist who is known and distinguished (for me it would be more correct to say "enlightened"), following the accurate reporting of his device, he sends an electrical impulse, calculated for each patient, to the painful part, always passing through the spinal column. In this way he frees the nervous system of its hitch and thus solves the problem of pain.

Below are the benefits I received after the two treatments carried out by Prof. Corbucci with the electronic equipment he patented twenty-five years ago.

Knees

I had made the decision to have surgery the next winter because I had gotten to a point of great difficulty walking, and it was even worse when going up and down stairs. I had severe pain in my weak muscles and tendons. I also very often had swollen and painful veins. My body compensated automatically when walking, and I soon found myself with one knee always bent, which I could not straighten at all.

I got down from the bed after the first application with my knees measuring less than ten centimeters and twelve centimeters in size respectively! Also the entire width of both legs was greatly reduced in volume, and I noticed that groups of veins behind the right knee (which were very visible and ugly) had disappeared! Prof. Corbucci explained to me that he had brought the venous system to an optimal state! In fact, I felt my legs were lightweight like never before, and above all, I could bend my knee and was walking without pain! I could not believe it. It seemed impossible to have such a result in such a short time!

Heart Chakra—Fourth Chakra (see page 12 for brief notes on chakras)

Then I explained to Prof. Corbucci that I had a strange cough, which had been left over after so much spiritual work. That work had improved the problem a great deal but was not able to cure this problem entirely. According to the professor, it probably had something to do with the lungs or the sternum that was perhaps pressing a little on the lungs, but only the machine would allow him to figure out exactly where the problem was. He passed the sensor along the spine, and all was well until it came to my shoulder blades. The sensor went crazy and signaled an anormality in the center of the shoulder blades to the left, exactly on the heart chakra! As soon as he inserted the needle at the point identified by the machine, I started crying uncontrollably while I visualized my early childhood. At the age of two years old, I was left in the care of my grandmother by my parents, who immigrated to England to work. It was 1950, and the world was recovering from the last terrible world war. The Italian government had signed with the English and Belgian governments a collective contract: in exchange for Italian labor, England and Belgium were offering raw materials, like coal and steel.

My parents left both myself and my younger brother of sixteen months with our maternal grandmother, the extraordinary Maria. Unfortunately she could not take care of both of us and at the same time get on with the farm with its twenty and sometimes thirty laborers, in the province of Benevento. So with the help of the village priest, Grandmother Maria was able to send me, on a very exceptional basis, for care in a sisters' convent in Avellino, where I remained for two and a half years. I did not notice the separation from my mother because for the first few months after her departure, I was with my grandmother and uncles (my mother's brothers) at the farm.

When they took me to the convent, I did not realize immediately what was happening, I was very sad to leave my grandmother, but I did not cry when my uncle took me to the convent or when he said good-bye and left. I did not cry on that day or for all the two and a half years that I was there. I remember very well that I was often very sad and melancholy and extremely in need of affection, but I do not remember ever even thinking of my mother in those moments (female aspect, the left of the heart chakra). When I used to feel so deeply sad, I would go for comfort to a nun with whom I had more confidence, one who embraced me more. I would sit on her lap and let her pamper me, resting my head on her soft breast (on her heart chakra!) until the sadness passed.

While Prof. Corbucci performed his work in between my shoulder blades, I relived it all, letting out all the pain and tears not expressed then and not even after! All those tears remained locked in my heart rear chakra for all those years!

Prof. Corbucci meanwhile was baffled by my tears and did not understand. He asked several times if he had to stop the session, if there was any problem. I tried, through my uncontrolled tears, to reassure him, urging him to continue since my tears had nothing to do with his mechanical treatment. Instead, he had rendered me a great service with regard to my energy field. He had unlocked my heart chakra, the fourth rear chakra! Obviously he asked me what I was talking about, and I tried to explain, between sobs, that we have seven wheels of energy that are conical shaped, of which one was the heart chakra, right where he had worked. He nicely asked me how I knew, and I told him it was not my personal knowledge but a knowledge that comes to us through five thousand years of Indian yogic practice.

"Yes," said the Professor, "five thousand years ago they did not need to go to college to learn about the human being."

"Indeed, the ancients had a great knowledge of man, just like you, Professor," I answered.

For that day, the emotions released were enormously profound, so we decided to suspend the investigation of the spine to a second session two days later. I went back to my room and went on releasing those emotions, which had been repressed for so many years, with uncontrollable tears. Then I fell asleep, and when I went down for dinner I was feeling much better, even though I felt somewhat strange, different and lighter.

Two days later the Professor repeated the procedure by investigating again with the "probe explorator" my spinal column and came to the Fifth Chakra behind my head, also known as the throat chakra. What had happened two days before with the Fourth Chakra was a total surprise for me, and although I had known for years that I had a problem regarding my throat chakra, I was not fully aware of what would or could happen with the Fifth Chakra when the doctor would get to that point. I had already worked on my chakras a lot during previous years with great results. I had unlocked the Fifth Chakra during the process and improved my cough a lot, which in the early years was truly an endless torment. Having said this, I did not expect what happened next.

Amongst my main problems, I informed Prof. Corbucci of a labyrinthitis, or Ménière's disease, which I had suffered last year and which had left "trails" and minor problems up until that day. Before he even began exploring Prof. Corbucci explained that Ménière's syndrome is very rare, and that most likely it was arthritis of the neck bone. He began exploring higher on the vertebrae of the neck, starting at the shoulder blades, and everything went well until he got to the very first vertebra. Again the probe signaled a fault or problem of my neurological system, precisely at the two sides of the first vertebra, at the base of the skull.

Like he had done during the two previous days, Prof. Corbucci inserted needles in the exact spot indicated by the probe of the machine, and again I began weeping uncontrollably. He had "unlocked" the throat chakra, the Fifth Chakra, the source of my endless cough never resolved completely, although much improved as a result of the many healing routes I had taken. This time I had no visions, but I was in more shock than the previous treatment, and I just could not control myself. Once again, the Professor was very worried about me, he could not understand what was happening. This time he wanted to end the session, but I insisted he continue. I explained that during an Essen therapy, starting from the Second Chakra and continuing through to the Fifth Chakra, I had had three regressions in past lives. Almost certainly he had finished the job that had been started then (about twelve years ago) of cleaning and balancing the chakras. He released traumas that were stuck in the Fifth rear Chakra. I had received the Essen treatments only on the front chakras.

Here I have to refer you to the chapter dedicated to Dr Giuseppe Calligaris in the second part of this book, entitled "A Spiritual Journey", and the chapter dedicated to the regressions in past lives to better understand what we are talking about with regards to the Fifth Chakra.

The first two treatments with Prof. Corbucci have changed my person, in my physical body, in my energy system and in my Spirit.

Physically, I had the following benefits:

- My knee pain was completely eliminated and I resumed a correct walking posture;
- My swollen veins of both legs were completely normalized with an immediate and subsequent reduction of the width of the right knee by ten cm and the left knee by twelve cm.;
- Almost total elimination of a persistent cough that had lasted for almost twenty years;
- Total elimination of a very strong arthritis of my neck vertebrae, of which I had been unaware. It did not manifest itself with the usual symptoms. Instead, last summer it broke out violently and was confused with a strong labyrinthitis;
- Immediate improvement of my vision by 0.25;
- Improvement of mobility of my hands (I had been suffering of arthritis for the past several years) and was suddenly able to close my fingers into a fist again.

Benefits of the energy system:

- Unlocking of the rear heart chakra, Fourth Chakra
- Unlocking of the throat chakra, Fifth Chakra
- Improvement of the overall energy flow

On the way back home, the same day of the second treatment with the Professor, I realized that I had even a different voice! The treatments had somehow affected my vocal cords too!

As soon as I got home I got rid of all the supplements and the two drugs I had been taking for a few weeks, the Arcoxia for pain in the knees and Vertiserc for the symptoms of "labyrinthitis" that occasionally recurred, upsetting in turn my family for "excessive behavior"! In fact, being a "decision maker", I had simply turned to a new page! I kept only the isoflavonoids prescribed by my gynecologist at the time of my menopause.

I had to learn to walk again, rehabilitating my legs and my body to the "normal" movement. I had to find the correct posture of the spinal column to avoid further damage. My energy was gradually normalizing, calming the great emotion that had been caused by the release of the chakra, but it took several days.

For other members of the family, apart from my husband, it was difficult to understand the level of pain I had before and the consequent great relief I felt after receiving those treatments, even though I walked slowly. They probably thought that it was all "in the head", both the pain and great discomfort before treatments, and the "healing" after. In reality, the treatments with the electronic device have given me back ten years of my life, I feel the same as when I was really in very good health. Over the last ten years it happened, at the beginning rarely then increasingly more often, to have a sense of ill-being, sometimes up to the point of almost feeling faint, other times it was enough for me to sit down for a moment and maybe drink something for it to pass; other times I had to just lie down. No doctor was able to tell me why.

That arthritis of my neck instead of manifesting itself downwards, with pain on the neck and shoulders, or with stiffness when turning my head, as happened to most people, in my case remained stuck there and travelled upwards towards the ears and the labarynth, thus hiding its true identity. Among other things having no pain in the entire area and not ever suffering from headaches was deceiving. For this reason, I never treated myself with Reiki on the head, and I never allowed any of my students to touch my head during the "multiple" Reiki exchanges. That part of my body I only treated myself directly, only my Reiki Master was allowed, no one else could even touch my higher chakras. This meant that my neck arthritis so subtly hidden was never treated with Reiki!

CHAPTER 2

Similarities between Science of the Future (M. Corbucci) and Ancient Knowledge

The parts in italics are quotes taken from the book of Prof. Massimo Corbucci, entitled **"The Physics of Chance"**

- *"The atom, shown in Figure 8 are concentric circles, representing all levels, are related to each other as are the frequencies of the seven musical notes, and are of seven bright colors, red, orange, yellow, green, blue, indigo and violet . "* They are exactly the colors of the seven chakras !! In addition they are also in correct order with respect to the chakras, from the first to the seventh chakra, according to the ancient Yogic culture! The "circle" is considered in all ancient cultures as "sacred", even in the Egyptian, American Indian, the Incas, Tibetan Buddhism, Zen and Theravada cultures! I think it is important as well as being very attractive for all Reiki practitioners, Shiatuzu, crystal therapy, yoga instructors and all operators in general that are minimally involved or working with the energies to <u>know that there is finally this scientific confirmation</u>. Until now we were all used to turning to the ancient Eastern cultures for any reference regarding the chakras. Finally a scientist of our times, a Westerner and Italian, gives us this truth, a "technical" explanation so important, while accompanying us towards a better future. I found it amazing to hear from this scientist and nuclear physicist the confirmation to that millennial knowledge handed down from ancient Masters who up until now were the only reference that we could use, without knowing for sure if it was true, but believing because it was transmitted to us by the ancient Sages . Today we are certain "scientifically" that the chakras are really seven, that they are made up of seven colors, and also that the order of the colors is correct. What a wonderful gift.

Brief Notes on Chakras:

In Eastern traditions, the human body consists of many energy levels, both physically and much "thinner" types. Buddhist scriptures evidence the notion that we are creatures with a physical body - which we use to run, walk, eat, and simply be in the world - but our existence is not limited to this obvious physicality. We also have a **subtle body** called "Body of vajra" (*vajrakõya*), adjusted by flows of subtle energy distributed along channels (*nadi*) and in energy centers (*chakras*). The energy that accumulates in chakras allows us to have and to be an intellectual, both emotionally and spiritually.

Chakra in Sanskrit means "wheel" or "circle" and indicates an irradiance of rotational movement. The most accepted definition refers to the chakras as energy centers that receive and distribute to all levels of the individual (body, mind and spirit) the flow of the life force (*prana*) that sustains life to which every being in the universe is connected .

The main chakras are seven, from the bottom up, from one to seven, they are called:

First Chakra: Muladhara: root chakra, our connection with Mother Earth, coiled at the base of the spine where the Kundalini dwells, holding us to the Earth by enfolding downwards into Mother Earth;

Second Chakra: Svadistana:, two inches below the navel, sexuality, creativity and, in females, the seat of all emotions;

Third Chakra: Manipura: level of the physical stomach, sacred space, confidence, self-awareness, will power, the right to be on the earth and, in males, seat of all emotions;

Fourth Chakra: Anahata: level of the physical heart, infinite love, compassion, openness to others, home of benevolence towards all living beings;

Fifth Chakra: Vishuddha: level of the throat, expression of all kinds, where the creative and artistic talents are expressed, also home of the verb, seat of the un-expressed verbal emotions;

Sixth Chakra: Ajna : forehead, placed in between and just above the eyebrows,seat of our intuition, allows us to perceive and understand everything that the physical eye does not see and or understand, also called the eye of the Soul;

Seventh Chakra: Sahasrara: known as he Lotus of one thousand petals, connecting us to the Universe and All That Is .

Chakras do not have a physical part or aspect but are conventionally positioned along the axis of the spine, and from the second up to the sixth, chakras have a front or anterior and a back or rear part. The lower chakras are considered closer to the earth and are related to the more practical aspects of life and its dynamics. The upper chakras are connected to the areas of mental, intellectual and spiritual aspects.

The condition of each chakra reflects the state of the corresponding physical body area. These energy centers are connected to the seven endocrine glands, exercising control of the hormonal physiology of the body, our behavior and our moods. In this sense man is a kind of energy chain, a vital bridge between Heaven and Earth, between low and high, between the physical and the mental, between material and spiritual, and the chakras pick up all their energies.

- The East Indian tradition describes the seven chakras as lotuses with different numbers of petals, which move in a circular motion at various speeds. The swirling motion develops at different frequencies emanating vibrations of light and sound based on the level of the corresponding chakras, seven are the colors of our main chakras, seven are the colors of the rainbow and seven are the musical notes!

- The functionality of the chakras is influenced by endogenous situations, which can unbalance and slow down their movement, changing their vibrational level, the cell exchange, the hormone fall along the endocrine axis and the psycho-physical balance.

- *"Gravity is indeed a great mystery"* and *"The gravity is there but it does not exist ":*

These are two quotes by Prof. Corbucci. In fact, he says : *this will surprise readers, but it should attract the attention of all that group of physicists, who are literally going crazy because despite gigantic and sophisticated equipment, installed to detect gravitational waves, they still have not revealed the slightest "space disturbance" as a result of events of large proportions, despite a kind of ... gravity. From the Sun we actually receive bursts of photons employing eight minutes to reach our eyes, while there are bursts of gravitons designed to hook the Earth to turn it round in the Solar System. Sun and Earth are "hooked" but not outside! The "free gravitational movement" takes place not in outer space, but in that "place" unprecedented in Physics, defined by an Italian physicist (Massimo Corbucci) QMV (QuantumMecahnicalVoid).*

In yogic Indian culture it is believed to be the first chakra, called "root chakra" that keeps us anchored to Mother Earth (and not as is normally believed, the gravity of Newton!).

- *To come to understand that a moment before the origin there was already what has allowed the explosion of happiness, makes the difference. To say it scientifically, or rather clinically, by a laboratory technician of Physics, "even before the birth of the Universe there was already gravity"*

- *"When the atom was "created" 13.72 billion years ago, due to the "sound" of biblical memory (at the beginning there was Heaven and Earth and Sound); there was the issue of sound and pauses".* I recognize myself so much in this statement because it touches a very deep truth within. During my courses and especially during Humanistic Reiki exchanges I often make participants do a meditation with the 'OHM, or an OHMCAR of seventy invocations. I explain that BEFORE matter there was sound, as our Bible quotes, and that over the millennia East India believes that the "OHM", or "AUM" is precisely that first sacred sound! But Professor Corbucci goes a big and brave step further and says, *"At the time of the Creator's Sound (the "Fiat" of Latin, from which the "breath of creation" in tune with (by assonance) with "breathing") was the real Sound itself which gave that "un-materialness" which allowed it to become "visible." While from the "pause" derives that materiality that is so dear to St. Thomas, the Apostle, who put his finger in the wounded side of Jesus because he was not content to just look at it!* Excuse me, but how pleasant is it, if not simply wonderful, to hear a <u>different scientific explanation </u>from that theory that wants mankind descendants from apes/monkeys? Finally a scientific explanation of the creation of "man, as Body and Soul". That section of the material and the spiritual issues regarding the origins of mankind, up until now denied by the "scientific" world, finally declared openly by a scientist!

In the Vedas (the Hindu Sacred Bible) (*Brhadaranyaka-Upanishad* (I, 2,1; I, from 4.1 to 5 and 17), *Aitareya-Upanishad* (I, 1,1-4), *Taittiriya-Upanishad* (II, 6.7), it is said : The following texts (*Vedanta*) repeat the ancient teaching of the *Vedas* (or, to be more clear of *Samitha*), and help us to understand it more deeply. At the very beginning there was no Earth or living man or animal, everything as yet was not. The text of *Upanishad* says that in the beginning there was only death and hunger, and that hunger is death. This simply indicates that we are still at the level of non being, and that the being is yet to be generated, but it specifies this equality simply because it is useful to understand why the deity Prajapati is sometimes described as an eater of food, a great devourer. The creation is intimately linked to the rise at the beginning, first, of self-consciousness. In the beginning, there was nothing outwards of "S" (the big S is = *atman*), in the form of man. This only form finally said "I am" (*Aham asmi*); or finally awakened the "self-consciousness." Thus was born also the first name of "man", man's particular individuality and that all now inhabits the world: "I". So also according to the "Upanishads" of the Vedas, we are not descendants of apes!

"*In nuclear physics there is a fundamental concept, that relates to the manifestation of matter or form wave or particle form. In fact, from the atom exits light, of 7 colors, in the form of photons, making the paradigmatic wave aspect of atomic levels, paradigmatic of "materiality" atomic* . This statement also is music to my ears because since many years I try to transfer this truth, known to me only by what is transmitted to us by the ancient Sages and by way of personal instinct that everything in the Universe moves in the form of vibration, in resonance or dissonance with something else. How can we forget the beginning of the Gospel of John: " In the beginning was the Word, and the Word was with God, and the Word was God. The same was in the beginning with God. All things were made through him; and without him was not anything made . " <u>Where "the word" must be understood as a vibration.</u> That primordial vibration, that the Vedas call AUM and that according to their teaching permeates the whole universe, existed before time and is at the base of all creation. And that vibration, identified with nothing but with emptyness, another was not and is not but the "Absolute". Here is the description of the birth of the Universe given by the *Vedas (Rig Veda X.129):*

"At that time there was neither existent nor non-existent.
There was no air, nor the sky which is beyond.
What was in it? Where? Who protected it?
There was water, unfathomable, profound.
At that time there was neither death nor immortality.
There was no sign of the night or of the day.
The One breathed without breath, with his own power.
In addition to that there was nothing else.

- In the beginning there was darkness hidden by darkness; indistinguishable, all this was water.

- What was hidden from the void, the One, coming into being, was built through the power of the ardor."

- *"I finally understood the inscrutability of Creation in the minds of those physicists, who refuse to open their hearts to the incontrovertible evidence that the most dense substance in the universe is thought . "* How many times in the different paths that I have taken in the past I reiterated that "the thought creates form". How much I have tried to pass this concept to my students! A concept that we find also in our prayers, two thousand years old, as well as in other ancient cultures. Emotion is energy in motion. When you move an energy, you create an effect. If you put enough energy into motion, you will create matter. Matter is conglomerated energy. Moved from here to there. Compressed together. If you manipulate energy long enough in a certain way, you obtain matter. Every Master understands this law. This is the alchemy of the Universe. It constitutes the secret of all life. Thought is pure energy. Whatever the thought, it is creative. The energy of thought never dies. Never. It leaves our being and heads towards the Universe, and extends forever. A thought is forever. All thoughts coalesce; all thoughts meet other thoughts, crossing in an incredible maze of energy, forming an ever-changing pattern of indescribable beauty and of incredible complexity.

Each energy attracts a similar type of energy, forming small energy entities of the same genre. When these similar energy entities bump into each other, they join together. It takes an unspeakably great mass of that energy to form matter. The matter is made from pure energy. In fact, this is the only way it can be formed.

Once the energy has become matter it remains such for a very long time, unless its construction is not demolished by a form of energy to the contrary or dissimilar. This dissimilar energy, acting on the matter, in fact, will dismantle it, freeing the raw energy with which it was formed. This, in simple terms, is the theory behind the invention of the atomic bomb. *Einstein* came closer than any other human being to explaining the secret of the creation of the Universe. It can thus be better understood how similar minded people are able to work together to create a very privileged reality. The phrase: "Whenever two or more are gathered together in My name ... " becomes more significant. Naturally, when entire societies think in the same way, very often astonishing things happen, and not all necessarily desirable. For example, a society that lives in fear very often, in fact, and so inevitably, gives shape to what they fear most. Similarly, large communities or congregations often find the power to produce events considered miraculous by the collective thinking (or what some people call common prayer). And even individuals, if their thought (prayer, hope, wish, dream, fear) is amazingly strong, can produce by themselves such a result.

Taken from "Modern Science and the New Heretics" by Dr. Demetrio Iero:

All that is, is wave form, energy or information. That has a shape. Everything that has form is also "wave form". So everything that exists has a shape and a body, even that which is not seen and cannot be touched, such as music and thoughts. Today modern physics admits that matter is composed of energy, in movement, which manifests itself in the form of waves and when it is static, produces force fields. The electromagnetic waves including the cosmic waves, sound waves, to the more subtle energies, including those issued by the brain, are "waveforms". Animals, minerals, crystals and even some geometric shapes emit radiations. Each preparation or natural medicine has a "wave form" of the mineral, plant, animal that it comes from. And these waves are similar in shape to organs, the viscera, the body in its entirety. And also the shape of the premises of an apartment, as well as that of the furniture or of the mirrors create waves which will have positive or negative effects on humans.

They constitute the basis and main body of Radionics: the Radioestesia paraphysics Radioestesica and physics, along with the study of the waveforms related to geometric shapes. The term Radioestesia has two roots: one from the Latin Radius, which means "ray" and the other from the Greek "Aisthesis" which means "sensitivity, perception". In other words: sensitivity to radiation, to impulses, to vibrations, to emanations.

The Radioestesia also includes the study of Geobiology and geopatia and leads into the mysterious world of vibrations, subtle and not, of all that lives. And the science which, through "feeling" the radiations that every body and every substance emanates, allows us to discover what is hidden inside them, to know the location, the entity, the nature, the kind, the quality and the influence they exert on each other; to come to identify and to feel what for most people is nonexistent. However, almost all people can grasp, understand and interpret them more or less powerfully, and also use them.

It was defined as "the eighth largest force of nature," "the seventh sense", "a medium between matter and spirit." In the Soviet Union this scientific discipline is elevated to University faculty and in both Russian and American army forces there exists special Radioestesia departments. Therefore, it's all about learning to feel these vibrations. During all the meetings we will work practically, using appropriate tools, to investigate the vibrations including the rod, the famous forked twig used only by those capable. The new message of salvation becomes "feel and listen to yourself and others", regain its identity, recognize the true essence of everything. See reality in the true light. It will also mean abandoning the metaphors of pain and duty. No more crawling external sinners in the valley of tears, no more sheep necessarily guided by the Good Shepherd, no more black sheep snapped up by the wolf guardian. "Feel", "hear" the inner voice that speaks the common light source. Sheep, yes, but for the Golden Fleece. Servants, yes, but of life. Warriors yes, but of light. Warriors with a common faith, on the way towards a single goal, finally together again recaptured the Temple to swear the "New Covenant". Recapture the Temple, find the sacred scriptures of life, the pages of light obscured by men of the past."

I find it only right here to share with you my direct experience with vibrations. After about a year that I attended the third course of Dr. Demetrio Iero I stayed home from work to care full time for my grandson Alessandro. I had recently moved into the house of my daughter and my son in law, in Cornaredo and since I had left work and was at home I was sick all the time. I picked up everything that my niece Aurora brought home from kinder garden, colds, sore throats, flues with fever and so on, endlessly. It was a constant thing, one after the other! I was always feeling tired and fatigued. So it was that I asked the intervention of two experts from Demetrio's school. They did a test of the vibrations in my bedroom on the ground floor and found very low vibrations, according to them "impossible to survive in that room". Then they turned to the garden and tested the entire grounds, then again in the house and in the end they decided that there were two streams that crossed under my bedroom, taking away all the energy which I so badly needed. They decided to "do an acupuncture to the Earth" to divert the streams' energy flow. The procedure was to insert three long iron rods, with a diameter of about two or three inches into the ground in three points of the garden, leaving out of the ground half a meter of the iron rod. The part below the ground, if I remember correctly, was at least two meters. I can assure you that from that moment onwards I started to feel better, and a week later I had fully recovered! I have experienced an even stronger episode with vibrations, but I must refer you to the end part of the book to the section "Other Experiencies - The Vibrations of Prayer."

• *"Between electron seventy one and seventy two of the "electronic distribution" in the atom, there is a" hole" so small that you can look out in the immense Absolute Infinite, as could be done by going to the boundaries of the Universe and putting your head out. In short, I discovered that to go to the other side there is no need to travel so much in space, because it is what separates us from the "boundaries" of the Universe, because it is "inside" each atom, because it is the "window named "QMV" that leads there. Years later I invented the instant transmitter, the device which may become necessary to communicate with the Earth once there will be the technology to travel in the "wormholes" (gravitational tunnels) towards distant galaxies, millions of light years from our own.*

Dear Reiki Masters and Reiki Second Levels, finally, a scientific explanation of how the third symbol works! Is it not amazing? For years I have reiterated that "the bridge" that we create to do distance Reiki does not go towards the outside, into space, but it goes within us. The symbol, if traced and invoked properly, brings us into that space which is infinite and timeless. A space that is within us and yet is connected to the Universe, that is where we can make our distance treatment, called also "distance healing". Now I finally understand exactly how it works!! We finally have a scientific explanation to this ancient method of healing.

- The Superior Monk Julien Ernest Houssay, was born in 1844 in Cossè and died in Geneva in 1912. I am referring almost the entire paragraph on this important text that somehow relates to all those of us in search of the truth. The following is what Prof. Corbucci says: *The Monk Julien should be considered the true authority of "interpretation of dreams" as a scholar of the phenomena "metapsychic" and lover of the studies of neuro-physiology of Dr. Encausse. For the followers of the orthodox interpretation of dreams, he was Monk Julio. What had this Abbot understood, more than Doctor Freud? Science is not a competition, but it must be said that the biblical accounts offer certainly more insights and reasons for reflecting than do the analysis that Sigmund Freud made to his patients in his studio: "The key of dreams is in the Bible," wrote the Monk in his book "The Great Secret Book of Dreams". Julien Houssay approaches the "neuropsychiatry" with a vision at more than three hundred and sixty degrees. He studied, for example, the "Physiology of the Psychic", ie the functional organic bases that could* <u>explain how a "special subject" could "get in touch" with the dead</u> .

<u>Finally a scientist who gives credit to a researcher who pursues the study and argumentation, with courage, of a subject so difficult</u> for most people to accept, even today. How many of us Reiki Masters, and non, have had several experiences directly or indirectly with those who are already in "the other dimension"? Experiences that remain almost hidden as we cannot talk freely because this subject is not easily accepted and recognized by the most part of the population. How comforting to meet a scientist of our time that confirms the results of the studies of a researcher of such great value, while

giving contemporarily credibility to all of us in our small and, in comparison, insignificant experiences. Experiences that are, however, important to us and sometimes are even shocking! How beautiful it is to be understood at last and again to have a scientific answer to this very old and ancient problem!

Personally as a Humanistic Reiki Master I had two students that after the Reiki activations became psychics, in the sense and as the Monk describes. One began almost immediately (now more than ten years ago) to write automatically, also called channeling with a pen. Another person has become (recently) a clairvoyant and "sees" and speaks with the dead, just like the television series "Ghost Whisperer". Moreover she also sees all the entities which accompanies each one of us! If in a room there are three people, she sees at least six, sometimes many more! On the other hand they do say that no Spirit walks the Earth without being accompanied by an Entity!

"Do not be troubled too much if I tell you outright that the mind, the brain and psychology, as we understand it, normally have very little to do with the "phenomena" of dreams, therefore with all those night hours spent in the arms of Morpheus. So who is to interpret dreams for us if not the psychologist? To read a dream you have to know the alphabet that is not made up of vowels and consonants, as are words which are the expression of brain thought . It's a very special alphabet made of symbols . The symbol is a sort of "ideogram", with a schematic image that can summarize a lengthy sentence. For example, if under high tension wires you write "danger of death", there is no certainty that all people of the Earth are able to understand that it is better to stay away from there, because you risk your life. While, if you put a picture of a skull and crossbones below the wires, the "message"

25

arrives instantaneously, without the need for "translations". Well, we understand that the symbol is universal and its interpretation "shortens and short circuits" any grammatical, linguistic, even semantic notion. It goes right to the "heart".

All energy operators that use symbols and in particular Reiki operators and Reiki Masters, while reading this must be thinking of the symbols of the second level Reiki. They are ideograms of Japanese tradition, yet they work in all countries of the world, in any language! Their shape and form has its own "language" and therefore works independently, and goes straight to the heart as Prof. Corbucci says.

Prof. Corbucci continues : *Houssay studied in depth the work of Dr. Gerard Encausse (1865-1916, known as Papus) undoubtedly scientific, which had formulated a conclusion very enlightening: "What we call inner consciousness, unconscious, is surely the replacement of brain consciousness with the intelligence of the "sympathetic and parasympathetic system."*

Prof. Corbucci tells us: *Dr. Encausse, more than any other doctor who took an interest in "paranormal" phenomena, approached the "solution" of that awesome mystery that is psychiatry: the psychiatric ability of some people to "act" on matter psychically, to effect the functionality of the still unknown "enteric brain".*

How very pleasant it is to hear a scientist talk about the brain that is in the abdomen and not in the skull. That which travels with what they call "chi" in China. That which then travels along with Rei (forming Rei-Ki or Rei-Chi), that which reasons on its own and goes where it is needed.

Prof. Corbucci continues :

The structure of man summarizes the structure of the atom, and do you know what is the most "vitalizing" element both for human beings and for the atom? It is 'the "joy of living". The Etruscans (ancient population living in Tuscany, Italy just before and during the ancient Roman period) used to write on their bread with a bronze stamp "Utere Felix" (use with joy).

How many times have we Reiki Masters repeated to our students that the natural status of the Soul is joy and happiness? That you have to be in a state of joy to hear the Soul and to expand this type of vibration to the surrounding environment for the benefit of others?

- *Life is erotic. Happiness within the Homo species is an exception to the etymology of the word, with respect to all the other species. Man does not at all approach a woman with the purpose of re-production, but much rather for pure fun. Fun comes first ! God forbid if it wasn't so. The reason why the Universe was born is the same "trump card" that those beautiful ladies who, strangely enough, are called "whores", (in Italian "puttana") where "ana" means without and "putti" means children. They do not have children and this is what makes the happiness of mankind, who does not want to reproduce, but instead is epigonic of the motto: "First comes fun."*

All Humanistic Reiki Masters and all who are on spiritual paths know that the ancient technique of Tantric sex was intended to lead practitioners to enlightenment and did not have the purpose of reproducing the human species.

From the book on Tantric sex "Passionate Enlightenment" by Miranda Shaw, who says: "tantric practice is secret, you cannot talk about it. You cannot say, "I did this and that." It is absolutely forbidden". In this book, she does not report directly but considers her experiences in a new and deepened light, from both written and living sources. Shaw discovered a world in which women not only lived and practiced on the same level as men for their spiritual transformation, but, in many cases, even led the way. In fact, Shaw learned that for the serious male tantric practitioner, women were to be worshiped, honored and revered as the bringers of enlightened energy into the world. With this revolutionary reinterpretation of the tantric texts, Shaw was finally able to make sense of many of the seemingly desperate elements of this complex tradition; in doing so, she laid the foundation for a new chapter in the study of the theory and practice of Tantra. Miranda Shaw says: "Actually, I would say that I encountered the power and sacredness of being female, because the tantric teaching is that women are pure and sacred in the essence of their being. We are talking of the cells themselves, the energy, not just something you can achieve, but an ontological fact. This changes the direction of your journey. Also, my image of men has changed dramatically. I have found that they can be really decent, noble and enlightened. That they are able to deeply sustain the spirituality of a woman, and not only her emotionality. I discovered a type of male celebration of women which I did not even know existed. Finally, I was surrounded by images of divinity in female form, and seeing the naked female body in a religious context (rather than in a commercial and secular as in the West) has been deeply reassuring for me, as a woman. My understanding of what is possible in a man-woman relationship has changed, and with it the understanding of me as a woman."

In the Buddhist tradition, Bhairava wielding *Trisula* (trident) and shows a skull open and upside down, his back to the viewer; Kali, dark skin, wearing a garland of heads and supports a severed head showing the tongue. The couple, in an arc of fire, stands on the body of Shiva motionless on the flames. These three deities occur frequently in many tantric traditions: Bhairava, the Tremendous, is the destroyer of ignorance, the one who can give the impetus towards the knowledge; Kali, the Black, is an expression of divine energy, omnipresent and immanent principle "heart glory" of Shiva himself.

Their embrace, manifesting in all its aggressive potential, is a symbolic expression of the reunification of the human and the divine, man with Shiva, the latter being the final objective of all tantric monastic practices. Supreme bliss and absolute Consciousness.

• The void or "emptiness." Prof. Corbucci returns constantly in his book to the fact that the "empty" is not empty but "full", in fact it could not be more full!

How can we forget the definition of the vacuum of the Vedas which asserts how the void is nothing but the container of all the possibilities that may appear in one of the so called material worlds . In the Zen meditation one sits doing nothing but the ultimate goal is to achieve a vacuum or emptiness because there, one will find "everything".

Giuseppe Calligaris (Great Scientist and researcher)

Giuseppe Calligaris was born in 1876 in the province of Udine, Italy. He graduated in Bologna with a thesis entitled "The thought that heals", he moved to Rome to work with Prof. Mingazzini in the field of Neuropathology at the Royal University of Rome. He sacrificed a solid college career to devote himself entirely to his research that cost him several misunderstandings with his colleagues and other professors. Prof. Calligaris demonstrated that the internal structure of the human body and the skin tissue that covers it are in relation to each other by ascertaining a hypothesis of the existence of lines and skin plaques that correspond to the mental state of the patient.

Each stimulation of a finger or limb of a patient causes the same reflection on the body and the same feelings on the spiritual plane. He wrote the book:

The Wonders of Metapsychics, by G. Calligaris,
Published by F.lli Bocca Editori, Milan, 1940, original edition.

He called them "linear chains of the body and spirit" because he experimented that a slight and prolonged tactile stimulation or faradic (electrical stimulation) of these lines evoked, in a reproducible manner, some physiological reflexes that were linked together, between internal organs, parts of the nervous system and the mind.

He died in poverty in 1944.

This is how Prof. Corbucci feels about Giuseppe Calligaris: *by "discovering these plaques", ie the skin projections of the brain that are "reflections" capable of awakening perceptions of time, "subjective" and in different eras, objective, he will remain the greatest scientist of human history. If someone was capable today of making widely known what he had understood in the thirties, our current "system" would collapse, because you would see clearly that it is based on scientific "assumptions" which are simply delusional.*

Now just sit back and look out of the window. Imagine being able to see, not cars passing by and motorbikes soaring, but rather carriages and noble people on horseback, because time, lets say two hundred years, is being projected in your head. But it could be two thousand and you would see the Roman chariots, or twenty thousand years, and in this case the vision would be even "prehistoric." It is not at all an unreal fantasy, because in a full-bodied triptych of volumes entitled "The Factory of Feelings on the Human Body" (G.Calligaris) it is <u>described the technique to "turn on" some so-called skin "plaques," related to neuro-physiological "reflections" which bring back to the eons of ages</u> . And the question arises spontaneously : "will it be possible also further into the future"? We know that the past, present and future are only words of convenience and that indeed <u>time is a "continuum".</u>

It was really exciting for me and at the same time comforting to read these words that <u>finally gave a scientific explanation to my regressions in three past lives!</u> I hope that these pages will be just as comforting to all those people who, like me, have had these experiences. They are unusual and extraordinary events, and even though they are as real as every other part of our daily lives, they are not understood and are not accepted by the majority of our society, not even by the people who know us well and or who love us most.

A SPIRITUAL PATH

Dear friends, the following are my direct experiences. Not possessing the absolute truth, I can only humbly refer and share with you, in a narrative form, what I have experienced personally, as incredible as these episodes may seem.

CHAPTER 3

The *AVATAR SATYA SAI BABA - 1998*

I have to start from the experience that has radically changed my life and my awareness. One evening I went to a pizzeria for a bite to eat before going to a course on the chakras like every Wednesday. I saw from outside, just before entering a young man dressed in green, army like clothes and completely bald, like a skinhead, who was speaking with the owner of the pizzeria. The young man had a white halo all around his body, from his head to his waist. I was amazed by this vision because I am not one of those people who see Auras. I thought that this person must be very special for some reason. Once inside the pizzeria I tried to figure out how I could talk to him without looking like the usual forty five year old trying to hook up with a much younger man. Meanwhile I saw that he had some video tapes of movies with the word "India" on the label and I thought to myself that he must have pursued spiritual paths in India and who knows what else as well as done many meditations to have this white Aura. Unfortunately he left while I was ordering and thus I lost the opportunity to make his acquaintance. I was so struck by this incident that I could not give up without first asking the owner who the young man was. She confirmed to me that he was indeed a special person, he was going to leave everything here in Italy and move out to a leper colony in India.

I have to take one step back here; one morning in mid-July of 1998 I woke up and I knew for a fact that I had to go to India but I had no memory of dreams or visions that could have happened during the night. As I prepared to go to the office I was surprised by this decision because I had no idea where I needed to go or why, but I knew for a fact that, that need, that feeling, was binding. As I drove to go to work I remembered of a friend who was going to India to Sai Baba's Ashram. I had seen, at another friend's house, who practiced Zen, a photo of Sai Baba and I can honestly say that I was not drawn to him in any particular way, as a Master, although in reality then I did not know the true meaning of the word. But I knew for sure that I had to go to India. I did not understand however why India considering that, since 1991 I went at least once a year, often twice, to Senegal, in Africa, at first to organize a convention, then to follow up on my projects of humanitarian aid that I organized personally on my own until I became a member of a Rotary Club. The club adopted the project and then extended it to other villages.

In the photo at the top of the page I am sitting on the floor during a thanking ceremony for all the food and vaccinations that I had brought in 1992. The photo above was taken with the village Witchdoctor and I am with a very dear friend John H. Fay of Sarasota, Florida, who in 1995 gave me a substantial contribution which I used, together with a donation from my very good friend Tommaso C., for the first trees. Here we are in the village of Yayeme Senegal where we discovered, only when we got there, that seventy percent of the population were and are still called Faye(!!!). Karma and destiny have their strange ways of bringing us right where we should be.

In the photo at the top of the page, during a meeting in the village I had "adopted" so to speak; photo on the right is the mother we met whilst driving in the Savana and whose baby had a severe infection of the eye, we discovered after she had stopped the jeep to ask for help. I cleaned it with a mild eye disinfectant and treated it with a specific antibiotic, locally. I left the rest of the little tube and gave her instructions as best as I could with gestures and heart and body non verbal language in order for her to treat the baby during the following few days. I don't know her name but I like to think that, maybe, we saved her child's eye.

As soon as I arrived at the office I called my friend and asked her if I could go with her to India. She was very happy at this request because she did not speak a word of English and had been worried because she was travelling alone. When I called the travel agency, I was told that all departures for India for the first days of August were completely sold out and there was no room. While he was giving me this information a colleague interrupted and told him that the day before three people had cancelled and there were now three places free. The Agency moved my friend to this flight therefore in the end not only did I find a seat for India but we even travelled together.

Lets return then to the evening I met the boy at the pizzeria. The boy had just left and I asked the lady if it was possible to know where exactly he was going, and exactly which was the leprosarium where he would be going to. Maybe that was the reason why I had to go so urgently to India? Had I to bring help of some kind to the leper colony in India and not only help Africa like I had been doing? I informed the lady of my imminent departure for India and asked her to ask the young man what they needed in the orphanage and the leprosarium where he was going. On the following Wednesday the lady of the pizzeria gave me the address of the orphanage, leprosarium and Mission in India, informing me that it was a missionary of a Catholic priest in Hyderabad. The orphanage was located in a leper colony built and organized by Father Luigi for the lepers who were expelled from villages and communities and forced to beg on the streets for survival, with their children. The father had personally collected around the world the necessary funds to build this hospital for leprosy patients that he picked up on the streets and took care of in his hospital.

Once these persons healed he taught them a trade, for example to build prostheses for their own missing or maimed limbs which had been consumed by leprosy. The women were taught sewing, other men to build houses, and so on. He gathered all the children from the streets, children of those lepers that had not made it and gave them shelter and an education.

After talking to the Lady of the pizzeria I thought that I *just had to* go to India to bring even a little help to that missionary Father and his sick people. So I went about obtaining from the company where I worked a donation of latex gloves, and from a Rotary Club (at that time I was not yet a Rotarian), many boxes of bandages from my good friend the Governor of District 2050 for the year 1996/7. Now I was almost ready to leave, but with a little concern about the weight of my suitcase. In fact I was counting on the fact that my friend would bring a suitcase with few very light clothing that would weigh very little and therefore I could hopefully compensate with my heavy suitcase.

Two days before our departure I dreamt of Sai Baba. Usually I never remember my dreams instead, this time I remembered very clearly the face of Sai Baba who was smiling at me. At that time my spiritual awareness had not yet expanded and I did not realize the importance of the event and did not yet know that you never "dream" a spiritual Master, but it is the Master who visits those he has chosen. I felt very privileged.

On the day of the departure I was very worried because the night before I had struggled a great deal to close the suitcase, at one point I thought I would never close it, even though I had sat on it! I had packed only a few cotton garments for myself, the rest of the large suitcase was full of gauzes, bandages and latex gloves. I prayed that I would be able to check- in at the airport in Italy by putting the two suitcases together on the scales and balancing my over-weight case with my friend's half empty case! Above all I prayed that while going through customs in India no one would make me open my suitcase because one, I would have to justify the strange contents and the amount and two, I would never be able to close it again. Fortunately everything went smoothly and during the stop between Mumbai and Bangalore, while I was waiting to take the train I was so absorbed in my thoughts that I did not notice the lady who was traveling with us and who was constantly watching me. She did not approach me at all even if (as I learned later) she felt very attracted to me for some unexplainable reason.

Once in Bangalore "our" car (there were several cars hired by the organization for the Italian group) was waiting for us to go to Putaparti and by chance the lady of the airport, who for convenience we will call Serena, was near us and she happened to join us as the third person in our car. When we arrived in Putaparti I talked to the driver and made arrangements to book the car to go to Hyderabad to the leper colony, three days later. Serena asked, in tears because she could not hold back the emotion, if she could come with us, explaining that it was more than twenty years that she had wanted to go back to visit once again a leper colony. She had heard that we were going and it seemed to her an incredible gift because finally her dream could be realized. Of course I told her that she could accompany us, it would be a pleasure, It was only then that she explained that ever since the beginning of the journey at the Milan Malpensa airport she had felt attracted to me without understanding why. Since then and throughout the entire trip she had felt this urge to talk to me without knowing until then, the reason.

At that point we decided to share also the same room with Serena and we settled, all three of us, in the guest room assigned to us within the Ashram of Sai Baba. The lights went out at twenty one hours, and at four in the morning there was the first call for prayers. Gradually, people from all over the world that had gathered in the Ashram would go to the large Hall to wait for Satya Sae Baba. All the women on one side and all the men on the other (as is the tradition for all public events and in all public places in India). Once we arrived there and before being able to actually enter the Hall we would have to sit on the ground, in an orderly manner forming forty long lines of about fifty people in each line. Then small disks numbered one to forty would be put in a silk bag and the line numbers were then drawn to decide in which order the lines were to enter. At seven in the morning there was the morning OHM of seventy invocations, called the OHMCAR, then at eight a.m. Sai Baba would enter the Hall.

While coming over to India, on the plane I had heard that it was very difficult to obtain a seat in the front row, once in the Hall and it could easily happen that two or three weeks would go by without ever being in the first few rows, or ever being called by Him for an interview for example. Now you can understand my surprise when, that very first day, our line was drawn second and I was able to sit in the front row! My mind was clear and my Soul was serene, I would say it was like a blank page, no expectations, no prejudices. I knew nothing about Sai Baba and believed that the only reason I was there was for the leper colony. Of course I was wrong.

Sai Baba came out of his apartment and walked down the red carpet which led through the crowd. He arrived right opposite me and then proceeded further. As he approached, a strong, emotional and mental change happened in me. I suddenly realized I was in the presence of a Deity, in the presence of the Divine. His great Divine vibration rattled my own little Divine spark, and my consciousness expanded and an awareness took hold of me. I was in the presence of the Divine incarnated for the good of Mankind, for the first time in my life I was looking at an Avatar. The emotion was really very strong and the tears flowed sweetly without my hardly noticing.

When Sai Baba returned to his apartment all the crowd came out neatly from the large Hall and my friends and I went out from the Ashram to go and drink our first cha (Indian tea pronounced as you write it). At noon we tasted our first Indian meal, inside the Ashram, strictly vegetarian and we rested in our room waiting for the Darshans (votive songs) in the afternoon. To pass the time Serena asked us if we wanted her to do some channeling with the pendulum, if we had questions to ask to the "Entities". Of course we were very interested, even if we knew not what was in store for us. Serena used the pendulum and a sheet with the alphabet spread in a circle of letters, after reciting a Hail Mary she asked the Entity some questions. We had all three sat around the only table in the middle of the room with the sheet with the letters of the alphabet in the middle and Serena held the pendulum at twenty inches from the sheet as she recited the prayer. Suddenly we all felt very cold (strange thing as it was very hot and humid) and Serena asked who was there with us, who had come to visit us. The Entity replied that it was my Grandmother Maria and, to prove her identity, explained that when I was a child I had been with the "women with long skirts and covered head, who dressed in black and white" (the nuns of the convent of Avellino, where my uncle took me when I was two and a half years) and that I should keep doing Reiki. She replied that yes, I should become a Reiki Master, because the practice was good for humanity but also good for "them." The story of the Sisters and the Convent was an information that Serena could never have imagined or invented, it was clear that the energy, the soul, the spirit, or whatever you wish to call it was actually there. I felt for the second time, for I had already experienced that kind of energy and presence (the first time was in England when I was eighteen), in my deepest self I felt the presence of my grandmother. I knew it was her and it moved me very much, I could not stop the tears much less ask more questions. Serena also knew nothing of my Reiki issue.

Three days later we left for Hyderabad and our elderly companion who was with us told me that she had brought with her five million Italian Liras to donate to the leper hospital, for she knew that Sai

Baba did not want and did not need donations. This was incredible, particularly considering that Sai Baba had had dug out seventy fresh water wells in as many villages. He had also built schools and universities in Puta Parti where young people could attend for free; he had built a hospital where one could go to be visited by a specialist for free. All hospital facilities were available and totally free both for locals and for tourists!

The journey was long, seven hundred kilometers towards the north from Bangalore, and the driver did not speak the dialect of the area of Hyderabad, so I often found myself acting as an interpreter when the driver had to ask for help to repair our car, which broke down three times during the trip. Fortunately it always happened when we were in a village and not in one of the long stretches where there was not a house to be seen nor did a car pass by nor did we meet anyone. It looked like a desert, with its red soil and sparse vegetation, very similar to the African Continent, almost as if to remind us that a few million years ago the two continents were joined. We had little food with us and there was nowhere to get us something to eat or drink in those few villages we did meet and where the car broke down. We saw unimaginable poverty and often saw squalid huts that were so dirty that we watched in amazement when we saw some "princesses" come out of them, dressed in bright saris and with beautiful braided hair and fresh jasmine inserted into the braid. We could not help but ask ourselves "where on earth did they get dressed? How did she put on the seven yards of fabric needed for each sari without getting dirty?"

On one occasion while we were out of the car and were waiting for the "miracle" that the mechanics performed for us by repairing the car on three different occasions, we found ourselves the center of attention and the whole village was brazenly watching us, to be more precise staring at us. There were two girls that could not take their eyes off of our sun glasses . Probably, as well as how we were dressed (continental) the fact that we were "white" caught their attention.

They may not have seen many outsiders or tourists either. Hunger and thirst were beginning to take their toll on us however. We settled for a couple of boiled eggs each that a man was selling, and tried not to notice the dozens of flies on the counter. Thankfully, the car finally drove off. We arrived in Hyderabad at ten in the evening, it was dark and there were no street lights. Our driver did not speak the local language and he spoke very little English, so we were a bit worried at that point. We were hoping to be able to find the building of the Father, known as the "white Doctor" some way or another, the problem was that there was no one around to ask for information. We did not dare knock on some home because it was already rather late, almost night and did not want to disturb people who one, probably had to go to work in the morning and two, with whom we could not communicate in any case.

At that moment I saw two boys on a scooter so I asked the driver (or rather I made myself understood) to pass them with the car and stop them. The boys came down from the motorbike and came towards me, I had got out of the car. With their very little English and my many gestures and body talk I asked them and pleaded them to please help us find the Leper Colony and showed them the pictures that the Missionary Father Luigi had sent me. The boys said they recognized the "white doctor's " hospital and asked me to follow them. Which we did quite willingly of course. However at first I was a little worried because they took us to a courtyard, came down from the scooter and went for a few minutes in a home; when they came out I asked where we were and they told me that they had stopped to advise their parents that they were going to take us to the White Doctor's hospital. They took another look at our photos and then mounted on their motorbike and led the way for us. We followed closely for about ten minutes, we dare not lose them, there was no street lighting and not a soul about the streets. They stopped in front of a building, which was an English School and the building was quite

43

different compared to the one in our photos. The boys looked again at the photos, then looked at me and shook their heads, it obviously was not our leper Hospital. They didn't seem discouraged at all and soon led the way again towards what they hoped would be the right place. Unfortunately this second building was large and quite impressive, but definitely not the Father's leper colony. At this point I began to feel very edgy about the entire situation; three women in a strange Town which was very dark because there was no street lighting, no shops or bars. I had only these two very young and willing boys trying to give us a hand, but with whom I could only barely communicate. Then finally, on the third try we arrived at our destination where we found Father Luigi waiting for us in the courtyard just inside the front gates. By now it was almost twelve, but Father was up waiting for us, rather concerned. He had had a dinner prepared for us which he said was frugal but given our hunger to us it seemed wonderful. I was so relieved to have found him.

I got out of the car and went to thank the boys and having nothing else with me, I wanted to give them both a very small amount of money as a token of our gratitude, as compensation for their helpfulness and kindness. Among other things for us the amount was almost symbolic but for them and their families it could be important, and maybe serve for something useful. I was rather stunned (to say the least) by their reaction and response: with his hands raised in denial, with broken English but very clear, I was told by both of them "no, no thank you, we cannot accept, because help cannot be paid for". I went back towards the house of the leper colony with a lump in my throat, unable at that moment to say a word. How conditioned are we in our society that such an unselfish and generous act catches us so much by surprise? And how wonderful is the principle "help cannot be paid for"? I will never forget this lesson of "Service to Others" without expecting something in return.

The next day our missionary Father gave us a tour around the structure. A workshop for hearing aids, an orphanage for the children of those leper patients that had not made it, a sewing room for ladies, an office, a chapel and the hospital in addition to the central house where the sisters lived, the office and private room of Father Luigi, the guests' rooms where we spent the night, and finally the large dinner and kitchen room.

Far away, but bordering the land of the Mission were the houses in the new village that Father had had built for all former leprosy patients. At the entrance to the hospital we were received by a doctor and two nurses (Indian sisters that Father Luigi had converted) and when we walked into the large medication room some patients kissed the feet of Father Luigi with obvious gratitude, thanking him for saving their lives. It was a very moving scene. They who had been like zombies, had had to flee from their own people, condemned to die of starvation and reduced to begging on the streets, now had the hope to live and fit into their new village and lead an almost normal life, with that part of the hands and standing on part of their feet that Father Luigi had been able to save. I knew nothing of leprosy before and discovered then that it affects the hands and feet first, sometimes also affects the nose, and slowly consumes the whole body. While doctors and nurses continued to effect the medications Father Luigi went out for a few minutes to take some medicines maybe. I could not avoid invoking some Reiki symbols and treating all the patients together there and then. So I sat in the corner and with my eyes closed and hands crossed over my heart chakra, I made my Reiki treatment, remaining in this position for half an hour. When I opened my eyes I found myself being watched attentively by everyone in the room, patients, doctors and nurses. They had all stopped what they were doing and were motionless, facing in my direction and staring at me. When I had finished and leaned forward in "Gasho" to thank the Reiki Energy, they had also all bent over, some had bowed even before me, they waited a few seconds and then, smiling, they carried on with the activities that they had interrupted. I do not think they knew anything about Reiki nor exactly what I was doing, but they had intuitively understood that I was doing something good and spiritual for them.

The next day was Sunday and Father Luigi invited us to Mass at seven in the morning, before we left. It was a wonderful experience, I noticed how Father Luigi spoke to the Hindus of Christ in their own language. In fact the entrance to the Mission was a large sculpture of Jesus with open arms and feet that were surrounded by a lotus flower. The Mass was celebrated sitting on the ground, as is common in India, with a low table for the alter and Eucharist and the Priest was also sitting on the ground. The chalice, the cross and other items required for celebrating Mass were all very simple, made of iron and not silver or gold and in a minimalist style.

After the mass we left for our trip back to Bangalore through the ancient city of Hampi. The return was much less difficult than going, if for no other reason, because the car had no failures of any kind. Hampi is an ancient city and we visited the ruins and the temple. Then we walked around the flea market and browsed over the stalls just for curiosity's sake, with no intention of buying anything. Suddenly a gleam caught my attention, it was a medal and, without knowing why, I was terribly attracted to it. I picked it up and looked at it carefully and I liked it so much that I bought it. It was a gold medal, perhaps the only one in the midst of all that old iron, copper, and various odds and ends. On one side of the medal there was a drawing of the OHM and on the reverse side a drawing of the Deity Hanuman, the Indian God of courage and healing. I was then second level Reiki and I considered this a good sign, something suitable and intended for me. We stopped to sleep one night on our way back with no particular incident and arrived in Putaparti the next day just in time for the Darshan of the afternoon. We quickly freshened up and rushed to line up, just in time to sit in the last place of the fortieth row!

The Ashram was well organized and in order not to have the women rush in all at the same time to obtain a good position in the front rows, it was customary for the security guards to make sure that the forty rows of fifty women were maintained and that the order for entering that had been drawn was respected. All the other people that had not been able to line up in the forty rows, was then allowed to enter. The lady who was to draw the number now shook the cloth bag containing the discs with the numbers, then walked over to the girl in front of our row and showed it to her, she had drawn our number 40 as first draw!! I couldn't believe that we were entering first! We crossed the threshold whilst entering the hall and it was like going into another world, the energy was so strong! We sat in the front row right next to the red carpet runner, with bewilderment and feeling very privileged! What a godsend. After a good hour had passed and when the other thirty nine rows had filed in and settled themselves on the floor in an orderly manner, all the others had finally started coming in. We then started singing, the Darshans. After maybe another hour, Sai Baba entered the large Hall at the bottom and started passing on the red carpet runner through the multitude of his followers making his way to the front of the Hall where the stage was. The men were all seated together on the opposite side of the Hall. I was sitting right on the edge of the carpet, where he was due to pass in a few minutes. I got up and I turned around, along with all the other people, towards him, and, as he reached where I was standing, our eyes met. It is really hard to describe what I felt, but I'll try. It was a look that went right through me, deep down as it approached and touched my Soul. I became oblivious of time and space. I joined hands on my chest and on my heart chakra and asked, in English, "Divine Master, may I kiss your feet?" In response, he smiled at me and stretched out his foot from his orange robe. His bodyguards, who had witnessed the scene allowed me to bow down and I lightly brushed and kissed his foot which smelled strongly of roses. I could have asked for an interview, (which is highly coveted by everyone) or give him a letter with my requests, as did so many people. Instead, as if in a trance, and with an inner urge stronger than my will, I made that request, so full of humbleness . They say that he very rarely allows people to kiss his feet and when he does grant this permission, it means that he also grants a wish or a grace. I did not know this at the time and only acted out of pure instinct or "inner voice." I requested protection from all dangers for my children. There are people who go to Sai Baba's Ashram for two or three weeks for many years in a row without ever being able to approach him directly or to be interviewed by him, I was given this great privilege for which I will be eternally grateful. They say he grants wishes and gives interviews to those who need it most, or according to a higher plan, unknown to us. What is a certainty for me, is that this encounter changed my life forever.

The following days of our stay in the Ashram were quiet with no special major events. During our trips outside the Ashram we happened to come across a shop where they sold malas (like a rosary of 108 beads) made with different types of stones, I purchased several, both made of Rushka (the hard seed considered sacred in India) as well as of various crystals, amethyst, jade, rock crystal, etc. At one point I saw a dark medal, ugly really because it was of a very blackened silver but which for some reason really attracted me. It was laying in the farthest corner of the counter, I felt drawn to it like a magnet, so I asked if I could take a look at it, It felt very old and I wondered what could be its story. I asked if I could buy it, the shopkeeper smiled at me in a strange way (perhaps because, as I discovered much later, it was a Buddhist symbol of the Kalachakra and we were just outside a Hindu Ashram in a Hindu Nation!) He asked for an affordable price, so I bought it with the feeling of having bought a treasure even if it was in actual fact quite cheap and very tarnished. When I got back to Italy I wore the medal on a silver chain around my neck all the time, often wondering about its history. I decided to take it to my Buddhist friends, the monks of a Gompa in Viale Monza in Milan to see if they had any idea of what it was. The monks immediately asked me where I had bought it, or found it, or where it came from, because it had a symbol on the front and Sanskrit writing on the back, of the important Kalachakra ceremony. This is a ceremony and blessing that only the Dalai Lama in person could give no other Lama was allowed or able to ! They confirmed my feelings, it really was an important medal!

During the rest of our stay in the Ashram there were many moments of wonder on my part. One such moment was when I realized that everyone in the Ashram, but particularly non-Indians, kept breaking the golden rule when travelling abroad and especially in the Middle or Far East or Africa, which was to never drink water or other drinks that are not opened in front of the consumer. Instead, all the people in the Ashram drank the water that came out of a water distributing machine which was serviced by water from the general pipelines, placed in the courtyards of the Ashram. There were always lines of people who drank directly at the machine or filled their bottles which they brought to their rooms. At one point I also decided to drink that water, if all the other Europeans did it, then I could do it too, and it was the first time that I had broken the golden rule hitherto always respected in Senegal. I really appreciated the delicacy of the availability of freshly refrigerated water that the machine distributed, with the stifling heat, it was really nice. I did not have any kind of bowel disorder or anything, and when I returned to Italy my blood pressure was back to normal. I was not able to say for sure if it was for the water or for everything that happened in the Ashram, but in actual fact, I had no need to take the pills for high blood pressure anymore!

A few days later there were two sensational episodes which quite impressed me. The first during one of the times when Sai Baba walked through the crowd, an Indian woman asked more than once Sai Baba to grace her son and give him the gift of being able to see, for he was born blind. At one point, Sai Baba stopped, turned to her, and told her that she could not know what his son had done in a previous life that had led him to choose this karmic experience in this life. The woman lowered her eyes and fell silent and it was assumed that the child had in turn caused blindness to someone else in a past life.

The second episode occurred during the afternoon Darshans and Sai Baba was on stage at the far end of the hall and an Arab woman who was sitting not far from me suddenly was completely covered with vibhuti, the ashes which Sai Baba generates directly from his hands! She was totally covered with it from her shoulders to her feet, and in a moment all the Indian women and many European women literally jumped on her to get some Vibhuti. The woman burst into tears with great emotion and the ladies responsible for the safety of the Ashram had great difficulty to pull off the women from the lady who was covered and at the same time keep away those who wanted to join in and also take some vibhuti . Meanwhile, we asked in English to the Arabic lady what had happened, and she told us that she had been spending all that time mentally asking, Sai Baba proof of his divinity, when suddenly she had found herself covered with Vibhuti!

That experience in the Ashram of Sai Baba and meeting with him directly, completely disrupted my life. Locking eyes with Sai Baba made me aware of and gave me comprehension of my Divine Spark. His being an Avatar and being on the Earth to help mankind helped me better understand Jesus' role. The writings in his Ashram such as "serve all" made me understand better persons like Saint Francis and also my role and that of all men on earth. In his ashram, and in the great Hall for visits in the morning and in the Hall for Darshans in the afternoon there are, on the sides of the stage, giant images of the four major religions of our world, Abraham for the Jews, Jesus (not on a cross but a shepherd) for the Christians, the moon and the star for the Muslims and a large Buddha for all Buddhists; high above all these images, measuring about one twentieth of the other images was a picture of Sai Baba for the Hindus. An extraordinary message of humility and humbleness (putting his image much smaller than all the others) and unity of religious practices, saying, without saying, that all religions lead to the same place, the same God. That there is no rivalry between the various religions, giving a practical demonstration of the meaning of the word "tolerance". Sai Baba welcomes everyone, helps everyone and is at the service of all. During my stay I found many similarities with the teachings of Jesus. There were the photos (which I bought) where Sai Baba also fed the multitudes of people sitting in a row on the grass eating rice on a banana leaf. At that time, when Baba was very young, all the village was very poor. Sai Baba began by feeding them, and the pictures I had found reminded me of when Jesus fed the multitudes with the multiplication of the loaves of bread and fishes. In the Ashram everyone talked about the "rosary" of Baba and not the Indian mala and this Christian reference quite surprised me. When I saw the hospital and schools that Sai Baba had built I was very impressed by the great change that, alone, he had brought to Putaparti; he had fed them, given them a free education and then ensured their health, also free of charge.

During that stay I understood, from a Hindu, compassion and love for my neighbor and for others, which Jesus talked about and I had heard so much of during my life. Outside the Ashram I found a book that shocked me at the time, "Jesus Lived in India" by Holger Kerten. Jesus' unknown life before and after the crucifixion. It seems that during the "missing" parts of the known Bible regarding Jesus, that is from eleven to thirty three years when he reappears, Jesus lived in India. It also seems that Jesus returned to India after the crucifixion (and resurrection) with his mother Mary, where they lived for another forty odd years and where their tombs can be found. Possible hypotheses? Maybe. But then who knows what is the truth? I bought many books in the Ashram with the teachings of Sai Baba including "Words of Jesus and Sathya Sai Baba". I bought many CDs of music and a packet of vibhuti, placed in a paper folded in four to contain it and where "Ohm Sai Ram", the mantra of Sai Baba, had been hand written. This vibhuti was used by me on many occasions, and for many months. It was a small amount of twenty or thirty grams so it should have ended in a short time, however it came about that for a year and a half the vibhuti continued to regenerate, to reproduce itself. Every time I opened the bag I found it in the folds of paper, on the outside, where it was not before, when I had folded it and put it away.

Most important of all, I understood the meaning of spirituality, the sense in leading a spiritual life. An awareness that I will never lose again. Towards the end of the stay I was happy that I had never had the need to give Sai Baba a letter with my requests, there was no need for he captures all of our thoughts, which he then elaborates better than any server. I was happy not to have had an interview with him or talked to him with the group of Italian followers because I would have been ashamed if Sai Baba had materialized something as "proof" of his Divinity for someone in the group who had been skeptical! I did not need further proof other than all that surrounded me and to which I had the honor to participate and witness. I was amazed to feel the peace and order within the walls of the Ashram with 35,000 people from all over the world, of all ethnicities and religions, who, almost in silence and without any clamor or fuss, would move around in the Ashram carrying out the various functions and ceremonies, serving meals and going to their dormitories, following the rules that were supervised by the security force made up of almost all young women.

On my return to Italy it took a few weeks to completely get back into the old routine. I felt like I had been on another planet. From that moment I began the long search of my inner self. I had already attended for two or three years a Zen Dojo in Milan, and I must say it was a very significant and important experience for me, even if in the end I chose another way. It was in that period (1990-1993), among other things, that I met Reiki.

(Here I am doing zazen (Zen meditation) on a beach in Africa)

A few months after my return from India I went to hear Tibetan monks playing the large Tibetan trumpet in a ceremony to celebrate their new year (January / February) and when I entered the theater, a person, who was distributing leaflets, gave me one. It spoke of a trip which had been organized to the Spiti Valley in the Himalayas, in Northern India, on this side of the border with China. The great news was that the trip had been arranged in order to take part in the Kalachakra ceremony, which was performed by His Holiness the Dalai Lama in person! Perhaps the medal that I bought outside of Sae

Baba's Ashram was an indication for me, maybe I should make that trip. It was certainly a strange coincidence! I had never heard before of "Kalachakra." I felt a deep urge to participate and decided that this would be my next vacation and I would definitely take part in the Kalachakra.

CHAPTER 4

THE HIMALAYAS, AMONG THE PEOPLE OF THE RAINBOW AND THE DALAI LAMA

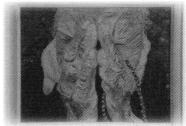

Young monks with photo of H.H the Dalai Lama, A Tibetan lady praying

The journey made to the Himalayas in 1999, thanks to Alexandro of a small but specialized travel Agency in Milan, passing through India, to the Monastery of Spiti, was the most extraordinary of my entire life. Our camp was at 4,500 meters above sea level, it was so unreal that it seemed that we were on the moon. But let's start from the beginning. I undertook the journey with great serenity despite the fact that I had never been to such altitudes. On the contrary my daughter was instead very worried for me because of my high blood pressure (even though since I had come back from Sae Baba's Ashram in India it was regular and I no longer needed to take medication to lower it). The first stop was in New Delhi, in an English ex colonial style Hotel, very pleasant, where we stayed only one night. The rooms, corridors and halls were huge and even had all the original furniture of the late '800s and all the atmosphere of that period was still in the air. It must have been a good life for the English Army and their families in mission in the English Colony, before the period of that one amazing little giant, called Mahatma Gandhi. Early in the morning a big bus, a van and several small jeeps were waiting for us with local drivers and tour operators who would later prepare all our camps, the first for one night only after we had crossed the first pass and the final one at the foot of the Monastery of Spiti. We were heading to Manali, our first stop, at the foot of the Himalayas, at 2.000 meters above sea level, and it would take us all day. It is known that in August there are monsoons in India, but I did not expect such an exaggerated dampness. We seemed to have absolutely everything wet, the clothes on our backs, those in our suitcases and even the sheets and blankets on our beds in the Hotel! I resigned myself to this unusual condition and settled into the bus. We soon set off in the direction of Manali leaving very early in the morning, glad to soon have the chaotic Delhi well behind us. At about ten o'clock in the morning a heavy torrential rain started and it accompanied us throughout the whole day.

We had just started to climb the mountains when right in front of us a mountain landslide plunged onto the road and continued its journey into the ravine. We could not proceed further, but we were so happy and amazed as well, at not having finished under the avalanche, that the fact of having to change route and having to go somewhere else to spend the night did not bother us at all. The bus had just enough time to stop with an abrupt halt before slamming into the mud and blocking the road completely! What a stroke of luck, or great protection! However you want to see it, we were all so relieved and confident that we could continue smoothly for the new destination relying completely on the organizer and local staff.

We continued to rise and the landscape changed a lot. Small villages and groups of houses were increasingly rare, giving way to lush green vegetation. The guide explained to us that those areas were once the destinations of the English for their holidays. The roads we were travelling on were very narrow and we were always on the edge of very steep crevices which made my head spin at every glance. Fortunately you could see little when looking down, thanks to the thick vegetation, we could, however, see the other side of the gorge, also very green, but not the bottom of the valley, so to speak. Every now and then we could see some temples and nothing else. All of a sudden I realized I was looking at the curve of a rainbow, in the sense that we were <u>over</u> the rainbow that had formed in the middle of the narrow valley or gorge! In some part of the valley it was raining, beneath us, and in another part the sun was shining, again, beneath us, forming this rainbow. It was a very strong emotion and a strange feeling, as if we were to become aware of the height at which we were actually travelling even if it did not look like it! It does not happen every day to be on top of a rainbow, instead of beneath or in front of it!

Finally we reached our destination, and although the hotel seemed quite nice, it was hard for us to sleep "in the wet", because at this point to say that the bed was wet would not even be correct, because it seemed that the beds had been made with sheets which had just come out from the washing machine, or rather had just been washed in the river! Likewise, the armchairs, chairs, floor and everything else!! Eventually we just accepted the fact that we would have to sleep in the wet, there was no choice! The next morning we took a detour and then the road to Manali, we had a long way to go and we would arrive only in the afternoon. The route was similar to the day before, narrow gorges and breathtaking cliffs with green vegetation with a few monasteries and Hindu temples on the way. It happened several times to see a rainbow "from above," as we approached Manali. The Tibetan people are also called "the people of the Rainbow" and now I understood why. Nevertheless to see rainbows from that perspective was really exciting and gave us a sense of the unreal.

We arrived in Manali with no other mishaps and we were met by a quiet and unexpectedly modern Town. Here the air was less humid, something for which we were very grateful. After settling in the hotel, which was pretty and unpretentious but with all the "comforts" usual for us Europeans (actually we were only Italians from Milan and rather spoilt. We went in search of a Tibetan Lama and his wife who I had met in Italy. There were five of us, out of a group of about twenty people, and when we found them they welcomed us with pleasure in their modest home and offered us tea. Their house was clean and fairly basic with very little furniture, but there was a good energy, and it could be felt. It was as if the air was purified of any impurities and permeated instead, with positivity and love. I had met with this Lama about six months before, in Italy. A group of Italian Buddhists had invited them over to Italy from Manali and by word of mouth they had spread the word of this visit to other Buddhists. For some unknown reason, since I am not a Buddhist practitioner, the news had reached me also and I had decided to go, along with a group of friends who were practicing Buddhists. The meeting was held in a "Gompa" in Valtellina. That encounter was a shock for me and, to this day I have no rational explanation for what I saw. The large room was full of people, men and women of all ages, many practicing Buddhists, others like me, driven by a strong need for research in seeking the "truth" or at least some answers. The Lady, the wife of the Lama, began to prepare for a ritual that was to be held shortly. I had not been informed of anything or given any kind of information regarding the purpose of this visit so I thought that she was preparing for a ceremony that would involve her directly and, strangely enough, not the Lama.

Several candles and incenses were lit in many different positions in the large room..

I was sitting in the second row so I could see very well all the preparation. The Lady was constantly reciting a mantra, during the entire preparation. At one point she was stricken with hiccups while she "dressed" with some special clothing and then placed a crown like headdress of many colors on her head. This sort of crown had many thin strips of colored cloth that hung down to the two sides of her head. In the Buddhist tradition they have the value of a blessing and represent the making of offerings. They are also a form of prayer. At one point the Lama stood up, he seemed to look around, then he opened a window to let in the Tara Divinity that would take possession of the Lady. The Tara in the Buddhist tradition is the Universal Feminine Energy.

After a few minutes, the Lady, while still continuing to recite her mantra, prepared herself at the center of the room, with her back towards the far wall of the room. She stopped reciting and nodded to the Lama, who spoke with the organizer who in turn approached some people in the front row and invited them to approach the Tibetan Lady. Along with them came a person who acted as interpreter. Three people were standing in single file, waiting for the lady to finish with the first, who was a young woman. I could not see what was going on very well because the young woman had her back to me but at some point I realized that the wife of the Lama was a healer! People explained their disorder and she acted according to the various situations. What happened before my eyes was absolutely incredible and extraordinary. I remembered having seen pictures in some magazines roughly ten years earlier in an article about the Philippine "healers" who worked with their hands. They performed surgical interventions by opening and closing wounds with only their hands. No instrument of any sort was used.

At that time, even though the facts were hard to believe, I still left room for doubt, one should see for oneself and then judge. And here I was in front of a person who did exactly those incredible "surgical operations." I was mesmerized, shocked but unable to look away. If I could have done so, I would have gone even nearer just to look more closely! I was sitting right behind the sick person, so I was unable to look right at her belly, but I could see well the blood dripping from the hand of the healer while she raised them and explained to the "patient" what she had taken out of her body. Sometimes showing parts of an undefined shape of I don't know what, other times showing a tangle of hair, sometimes even stones, and so on, as the people went to her one at a time. I sat or stood spellbound watching the long line of people who approached the healer for five or six minutes and then walked away. Some of them indicated to her their kidney, some others their abdomen, and others were complaining about something serious regarding their head. When the Healer had done her job I watched them leave, as they walked past me. Some with an expression of utter amazement others in disbelief and unable to speak for a few hours later! To be honest, I was almost sorry not to have had anything that needed to be cured, I would so much have liked that experience personally. The Healer put down everything that she had taken with her own hands, from inside people's bodies like their chest, the stomach, the backs, kidneys, head, etc. in a metal container. I was so focused on what the Healer was doing with her hands that I didn't listen with proper attention to what I was told by the organizers and therefore cannot remember now the explanation that had been given of what would happen to all that stuff later. I don't know if it was all burned or buried in the ground or whatever else, accompanied by Mantras of course. At the end of that incredible day we returned to Milan and the organizers explained to us that the Healer worked with the Divine entity Tara and that it was the Divinity that did everything through the person of the Healer, wife of the Lama. In our culture, we would have called her a "Medium" or "Psychic."

While we sipped our tea and sat on the floor leaning on large cushions with our cups on the very low tables, I saw again, like a film before my eyes, that unforgettable day. I watched the Lady who was so gentle and modest serve us tea and as she asked the interpreter news about Italy I felt plunged into another world once again.

We parted from the Lama and the Lady Healer with the hope of being able to invite and host them again in Italy. We returned straight to the hotel because next morning we had to wake up early to go to the first mountain pass, the Rotang, which was at 3.850 meters above sea level.

2000. Rotang Pass, 3,850 meters a.s.l., above Manali, my limit before having to take tablets for the high altitude.

Behind us in the picture above you can see in the distance the higher Himalayas and the plateau where we camped for the night. We had left behind us the green Manali and from then on we did not see one single tree, neither near us nor at a distance. The porters had preceded us with the jeep and had already prepared our camp which consisted of a very large tent to enjoy our meals all together and a dozen small tents where we settled into our sleeping bags for the night, two for each tent. We were covered in warm clothes, to also face and deal with the temperatures and height of the Pass, but after the heat and humidity of New Delhi four degrees during the night seemed very few and for us it was cold. The organizers had prepared a warm Indian soup and some lentils which were delicious. It was the first time in my life that I slept in a sleeping bag, even if very technological, and the first ever in a camp, in a place with no electricity, no roads, no mobile phone coverage and no structures of any kind. Where there was nothing, neither animals nor men, nor trees, bushes or greenery of any kind, and where the sky looked much closer and made you want to reach out and touch it, perhaps because, in addition to the earth below us, it was the only other thing there!

At dawn, the organizers brought us bowls of water, cold water, as the only way to freshen up a little before the next stage. They prepared some coffee and cha for us and to our surprise they had also brought some cookies and biscuits. While we were having our breakfast, after having packed our luggage, the Indian organizers loaded everything onto the two coaches and the camp was dismantled in the blink of an eye, leaving no trace whatsoever of our presence there. We left for the long journey that would take us into the Spiti Valley and to its Monastery, to take part in the Kalachakra ceremony . This ceremony can be performed only by the Dalai Lama in person and if someone is able to participate to three Kalachakras they will be sure to enter "Shambala", the ideal land in the Buddhist tradition.

The road was long and not without risks, due to the incredible ravines and cliffs on the sides of the very small roads, wide just enough to allow the wheels of our two coaches and our jeeps to fit, leaving only a couple of inches to the edge. The landscape had totally changed and we did not seem to be still in India. We began to realize that we were on the "top of the world" because everything around us was barren, no vegetation of any kind and there were only mountains, everywhere you looked, at three hundred and sixty degrees. Also we were having more difficulty breathing notwithstanding the tablets we had all taken for the symptoms that can be incurred when going to such high levels. During the short stops we made to stretch our legs a bit, we had to move in slow motion, it was not possible to act "normally."

One of our coaches, bottom slightly to the right, underneath we had an overhang that was twice the size of the mountain above us!

Soon we began to see the typical Tibetan houses and crossed a high plain, where the people who had fled from Tibet had settled, at about 4,000 meters, with the higher mountains all around. We passed in the middle of their fields and it was very pleasant because it all seemed so unreal. We wondered how it was possible that some people lived their lives normally so far away from any sign of "civilization" and how they survived throughout the severe winters so high up, with the many degrees below zero and all the meters of snow!

Typical Tibetan houses.

We continued on our way and the scenery once again became moonlike, we seemed to be thrown back to the Ice Age. Finally in the late afternoon we reached our destination. In the midst of this desolation without trees or animals we could see ahead, at our own level, one golden stupa which indicated the proximity of the Monastery, which could be seen looking up 500 yards to our left.

After a few minutes we arrived at our camp, which was ready and waiting for us. Local operators had already hoisted the large tents of conviviality, one was our eating tent and the other for all the other activities They had hoisted the smaller common tents all around, forming a circle, where we slept two in each tent. They placed two wooden "tables" for each tent where we opened out our sleeping bags so we were not on the ground, which we appreciated very much since we stayed there for six nights and seven days. The operators had dug six deep holes in the ground, not far from the general camp, surrounded by curtains that barely covered the circumference of the hole and which served as toilets. In one of the large tents there were plastic tables and chairs, it was our "restaurant", there was a large tent for the kitchen, where we were prohibited to go, and another large "open" tent for socializing together during the day and evenings.

The monastery of Spiti at 5,000 meters above sea level, you can see the Tibetan people and other Buddhists from Nepal and other Nations, who begin to arrive for the ceremony of Kalachakra.

As soon as we get off the coach and as we settled into our tents, I started to feel something in the air, something different from the world I had left behind. Perhaps it was only the thin air, or maybe it was the vibrations and energies which in that place were free to move around without being disturbed by "civilization." Indeed, as Prof. Corbucci says, *the vacuum is not empty but is full,* and indeed all the emptiness around us appeared and felt "full" of vibrations, energy and more. That night it was impossible to sleep, after dinner some of us retired to our tents, but most wandered about in the field on that high plain in disbelief, like me, with their nose in the air. I had never seen a sky so starry, so very full of stars, then someone told me that there was more than one milky way visible that night! The "expedition leader" so to speak, the organizer, prepared us a fire, digging a large hole in the ground and putting the logs of wood which the Indian organizers had brought with them, because we had not seen even the shadow of a tree after we had left Manali. We gathered around the magic fire, enchanted by the surreal atmosphere. It seemed possible to touch the sky by simply lifting one arm! We sat around the fire talking until almost dawn.

Our camp, bottom right, at 4,500 meters above sea level, seen from the Monastery which is 5,000 meters a.s.l. The white stripe is not a river, but the <u>river bed</u> !

The first morning was beautiful, sunny, with a crisp breeze and, as we did all the following mornings, we washed with a sponge brought from home and a bucket of <u>cold water,</u> that the Indian boys had brought to us outside each tent. Everyone, just outside their tent was preparing for this early task. The bravest were showering in cold water in a tent set up and used for this purpose. The water was then thrown a little bit away from the tents and outside of the circle of small tents so as not to wet and dirty the area of the camp. This morning ritual was followed by breakfast and then we all went, a bit crammed to tell the truth, in the two jeeps that took us halfway between our camp and the Monastery, the rest of the way was to be done on foot. His Holiness the Dalai Lama had already arrived and we had the honor and great pleasure to attend the morning prayers which he recited together with many Lamas. Many monks were left out of the Gompa, but we were luckily allowed to enter and be present, sitting in the space behind all the Lamas, who were sitting in three rows in front of and facing his Holiness.

Simply just sitting there and listening to the chanting of the mantras, allowing the sound of the voice of the Dalai Lama, followed by those of all the other Lamas, to penetrate our beings through the chakras primarily, but also through our hearing, was a purification and also an incredible healing event. The vibrations of the mantras of the Dalai Lama reached out to us and were felt very much on the skin of the arms and face, and through our eyes, it was possible to internalize the waveforms of the mudras of the Dalai Lama. The "mudras" are special forms created with the hands and being able to observe the hands of His Holiness the Dalai Lama, one holding the dorje, while reciting mantras, was truly an extraordinary experience. I was very moved and thrilled, and I could not look away even for a moment. This was the first of six days of preparation for the seventh day, when there would be the Kalachakra ceremony.

The more experienced and older Monks in all that time, during the six days, would prepare, working long hours, the great Kalachakra Mandala, and intricate design which is made with sands of many colors. This great work was destroyed at the end of the seventh day and at the end of the Kalachakra, to signify the impermanence of everything.

We stood there, glued to our places as long as we were allowed to. Unfortunately after a couple of hours we had to leave and no one else was allowed to enter unless it was a Lama or a Monk. We were not allowed to assist to the rest of the preparatory ceremony.

So we walked down the hill and I could not help but notice how easily the Tibetans came down, while we were forced to go slowly and were always out of breath! We met with our jeeps that took us the rest of the way back to the camp.

I remember very well the first meetings with the Tibetan people, as we climbed that morning. They all had interesting faces, both young and not so young, full of expression, marked by very strong sunlight and cold temperatures of the nights and by the long winters. They were smiling and friendly, they did not display any impatience with our presence on that occasion for them so sacred. The thing that struck me most was their eyes, clear and sincere, it seemed possible to read their heart and it was clear they had no need to prove anything to anyone, and this was clearly their attitude towards life. Their clear objective was only to be in harmony with the whole, humans, animals, mountains, rivers, and with everything that could not be seen with our physical eyes! It was obvious that they did not use, or rather not waste, their energy for malice or deceit or for what they did not need. Their energies were all used for their survival and to keep and continue the spiritual traditions of Tibetan Buddhism. They emanated an energy totally different from ours, and we could perceive very well how this energy was a continuation of the energy of the environment all around us and perfectly in harmony with the Universe. This happened every day, we went up to the Monastery, we listened to the recitation of mantras along with His Holiness the Dalai Lama for a couple of hours and then returned to the camp.

In the afternoon we were free and some of us went to the great camp of the Tibetan people, not far away from ours. Once we had got past the long lines of individual tents, one for each family, we found ourselves in an area of at least fifty of the great market stalls where all the Nepalese Buddhists had collected, as well as Tibetans. There was also a tent for "health care" where it was possible to see a doctor. We went there out of curiosity and were received by a very kind lady doctor who made a "scanning" or ultrasound of our whole body just by feeling our pulse. With a broken English she was able to identify and refer to us some disorders. We confirmed that these disorders had already been diagnosed at home. It was really amazing! She also prescribed some Tibetan medications, which we willingly purchased. The market was stocked with all kinds of goods and offered a kaleidoscope of incredible colors to the eyes. There were many stalls with beautiful necklaces of turquoise and pearls, which my friend bought. I purchased a money bill of Tibet, which is no longer valid of course, but I was fascinated by the possibility of being able to bring with a me a real piece of Tibet, which until a few years ago, belonged to the everyday life of that ancient world.

Banknote of Tibet, now in disuse

Wandering through the stalls we found ourselves without realizing it, in a tent with thousands and thousands of images of the Tibetan Buddhist tradition. Very large Tancas, medium and small paintings and images of Buddha in a splendor of colors to make one dizzy.

I could not help but purchase a beautiful Tanca of White Tara. While I was choosing it I thought that It was strange because we felt absolutely no kind of danger despite the fact that we were a handful of Europeans in the midst of hundreds, perhaps thousands, of Buddhists from all sides, many also from Nepal. We were unable to communicate with them except in gestures and facial expressions, ours and theirs! Despite the fact that the market was in full activity with all those hundreds of people that circulated among the stalls, an extraordinary peace reigned, it felt like we were in another dimension. Everything was as if muffled, sounds were sweet, smiles were always ready, the energies that reached us physically as we made our way through the crowd were infused with positivity, confidence and serenity. As if there were no thoughts or worries in their lives! The joy reigned supreme. I turned round more than once to observe the people when I heard laughter, that deep laughter coming from the "hara", that is, from the belly, it seemed all a game. Maybe we are no longer capable of laughing in that manner, maybe we no longer talk to each other as if we were playing a game, as children do.

Tanca of White Tara purchased directly from the Tibetans in the market of their great camp at 4,500 meters above sea level in the Spiti Valley .

One afternoon of those six days waiting for the Kalachakra we received the visit of some Monks who were friends of the organizer. Among them was a boy of about twelve years. We noticed that the other monks had a special attitude towards the child and the translator told us that it was because he was no ordinary Monk or child but was in fact the reincarnation of an important Lama.

Another afternoon we went to visit a monastery that was an hour away by coach. it was a very nice and interesting experience. The monastery was perched too (like the Spiti Monastery) on the top of a peak and to get there we passed some cultivated terraces, quite a sight after so much desolation and great spaces with a view for many miles away, without being able to see absolutely NOTHING. As we approached the Monastery we could not see a soul around, so it was assumed that all the monks were occupied in some ceremony. The organizer took us in anyway because, he said that he had obtained permission to enter during the previous days. He opened the door and invited us to go in but it was really hard to orient ourselves in the total darkness, especially after the bright light outside. There were no candles lit and you have to remember that there was no electricity!

Two of the few photos that we were allowed to take inside the monastery

In single file we continued down the hall, perhaps it was a room I could not see at all, following the voices of the monks, which guided us. They were reciting mantras in a room nearby. It was lit with many candles and lots of incense. Unfortunately I did not pay enough attention to the explanations of our guide and organizer, so I cannot refer much, because I was too caught up by the sound of those voices that penetrated every cell of my being. We settled down on the floor in the back of the room, near the door, the only place still free because the rest was occupied by the many monks of the Monastery. Their mantras moved very strong vibrations, perceptible by everyone and a woman of our little group felt ill. We made her lie down on the ground and one of the monks gave her something to drink. She recovered enough to go out and get some fresh air. Apparently the vibrations were too strong for her, maybe putting in "consonance" some parts of her body caused a reaction that she was not able to control.

THE MEANING OF KALACHAKRATANTRA

The following is a brief and general explanation coming from a humble person like myself who has little experience in practicing Buddhism and has only the humble purpose of trying to help the reader understand in some ways the importance of the ceremony itself. I hope I have been able to transfer what I have been taught in the correct and best way possible for my level of understanding.

The Kalachakra (kala = time, chakra = wheel) system belongs to the highest Tantric Buddhism (Mahanuttarayogatantra), and is divided into three levels:

the external level is the study of astrology associated with the elements, the oracular divination, numerology, metaphysics;

the internal level: is the study of the psychophysical energy, anatomy of the pranic energy of the human body (chakras, nadi and bindu) and of medicine. To strengthen and stabilize the functioning of the pranic currents (ie, the breath of life), and to raise the consciousness to enlightenment, practical visualization and mantra recitation are taught;

The third level is the deepest. Called "Alternative Kalachakra", it involves the teaching on emptiness of phenomena, the non reality of the self and of the Clear Light. The Yogi transforms the world into a mandala and identifies himself with the deity Kalachakra, an expression of enlightened nature, leaving the ordinary way of perceiving oneself and the world. Then the yogi works on the vital flows and their circulation in the body, leading to fulfillment of the reality generated by the power of thought and obtains the realization of the Clear Light, the profound nature of the mind. Time is without measure or purpose and is missing existence: the discovery of the secret kingdom of Shambhala is an inner journey into the Holy Kingdom, a huge eight-petalled lotus like the heart chakra.

TEACHINGS OF KALACHAKRA

Very rare teachers are able to transmit this teaching, and the Dalai Lama is the most qualified. Unlike other initiations of high Mahanuttarayogatantra, usually conferred individually or with a small group of disciples, the Kalachakra initiation is traditionally given to large groups of people, because the message of peace that comes from Shambala involves the whole of humanity.

Those who receive the inspiring energy establish an important connection to the mystical secret realm

CONNECTION WITH SHAMBALA

One of the reasons why His Holiness the Dalai Lama regularly gives this initiation is to be found in the prophecy which states that those who have received the Kalachakra Initiation will be reborn during the reign of the twenty-fifth king of Shambala, ready to obtain complete enlightenment through the meditation practice of this Tantra.

According to this tradition, now in Shambala the twenty-first king is reigning. With the advent of the twenty-fifth King, prophecy has it that our world will be struck by a conflict of enormous proportions; Shambala will also intervene in this war, for the defense of the just and for peace. Those who have established a connection with the pure kingdom will be warriors of Shambhala.

The significance of all this is that the message of peace that comes from Shambala invests all of humanity.

The Kalachakra Tantra is a practice of Buddhist meditation that belongs to the class of tantra of supreme yoga, the most profound teachings of the bodhisattva's vehicle. According to tradition, the Buddha Shakyamuni appeared as the Kalachakra in South India and taught this tantra on request of Suchandra king of Shambala. Later, the king Suchandra spread the teachings of the Kalachakra among the inhabitants of Shambala. It is said that these teachings and their practice reappeared in India only in the eleventh century, shortly before being introduced in Tibet. Since then, until the upheavals of the last century, have spread not only among the Tibetans, but also in the north of Mongolia, as well as Sikkim, Bhutan, Nepal and the region to the South and West of the Himalayas.

The Kalachakra is one of the last and most complex tantric systems introduced into Tibet from India. Unlike what happens in other tantra, which does not allow you to initiate more than twenty-five people at a time, to the Kalachakra ritual, traditionally the largest crowds can participate. The Kalachakra initiations are conferred on the basis of a mandala, the sacred abode with its resident Deity, usually depicted graphically.

The tradition I follow uses a mandala made up of colored sands, built with extreme accuracy before each initiation and destroyed at the end of the ceremony. It is important to understand the fundamental aspects of the Buddhist path providing the context within which the mandala can be used as an object of meditation. The first is the strong desire to put an end to the experience of suffering of ordinary beings. These range from the relative pleasure of the gods and humans to the pain and torment of animals, negative spirits or entities and the inhabitants of the infernal regions. The student must also feel a strong desire to achieve enlightenment for the benefit of others and to have a correct view of reality. Originally, the Kalachakra mandala was primarily associated with the kingdom of Shambala, that is, an entire community. Today, no one knows where Shambala is, but it seems that it still exists, even though we cannot see it or communicate with it in an ordinary way. Someone suggests that it is on another planet, others argue that it is a pure land. Whatever the answer, according to the scriptures Shambala will one day be back in touch with our world, allowing us to feel its beneficial influence once again.

While all the other mandalas regard only the individual practitioner, the mandala of Kalachakra involves the entire community, the society as a whole. One of the most obvious benefits that come from receiving initiation is that, even though not fully prepared, you establish a connection with Shambala.

Therefore, when Shambala returns and comes back in touch with the communities of our world, the effects will be positive. I also believe that to confer the initiation to a great multitude of people creates a strong positive link between all those who have participated, sowing and spreading fertile seeds of peace.

THE DAY OF THE KALACHAKRA CEREMONY

Finally comes the great day of the Kalachakra ceremony and in our camp activity began earlier than usual. We went very early to the Monastery because we knew there would be lots of people. I will not go into explaining what happened with regard to the Buddhist practice, out of respect for all Buddhists and for fear of getting something wrong in tracing back in my mind that extraordinary day, after so many years. I would like to share everything else though. While we walked the last piece up the steep hill, which took us to the Monastery we met very many Tibetans and Nepalese who had come for the Kalachakra Ceremony.

When we arrived at the Monastery we found the large square in front of it crowded with thousands and thousands of Monks and Lamas and behind them the population (also in thousands) who were climbing on the large boulders behind the monks, all around.

Above are two beautiful Tibetan Ladies climbing up to the Monastery for the ceremony. I was struck by the lovely colors and the quality of the fabrics.

We also found our accommodation to the side of the small semi-circle that had been left vacant for the performances and dances that the various populations had prepared in honor of the Dalai Lama.

At one point, some Monks went round serving everyone some "cha", (tea) which we very much appreciated. When the Dalai Lama came out on a kind of verandah of the Monastery that over-looked right on the main square, he created silence without asking for it and everyone listened very carefully and spellbound to every single word. It was very nice to see the intensity of their expressions as they listened to His Holiness. As I observed them, I noticed that many of them had their face turned completely upwards towards the sky, watching the sun which was directly above. I looked myself and I was astonished! Flat, around the sun there was a wide circle with all the seven colors of the rainbow clearly visible. How was it possible? I had never seen such a thing and I had never even heard of such a thing. It was right next and attached to the sun, flat and colored, right above our heads. As the ceremony went on, every now and then I looked up and the rainbow was still there. Many other Monks shared the task of bringing to all the thousands of participants, without exception, a red ribbon, about two centimeters high and about five centimeters in length, to be put on our face, during the most important moment of the ceremony, which would take place soon . Other Monks brought us a handful of rice each, which we also eat with appreciation. The cha, the ribbon and the rice were all very impregnated with the vibrations of the many Mantras that the monks had chanted since dawn. At this point the various shows began, first the sacred dances performed by the Monks in sacred costumes, then some actors (adults and children) performed a humorous sketch and finally there was the dance of the people of Ladakh. The rainbow was still there.

The Sacred Dance for HH the Dalai Lama immediately before the opening of the ceremony

The Tibetan monks in front of the Spiti Monastery, during the days preceding the Kalachakra Ceremony

The dance of the people of Ladakh in honor of His Holiness the Dalai Lama

I tried several times to photograph the rainbow but the sun was too strong and I did not have a suitable camera, or perhaps simply did not know how to take that particular shot. I was really sorry though, I would have really wanted something as witness and testimony of that rare natural event.

At the end of these spectacular shows, at that point late afternoon, the Dalai Lama spoke again with his people and with everyone else present and then returned inside the Monastery, at that moment I looked up and the rainbow had disappeared! What a strange "coincidence". The organizer informed us that the ceremony was over and the great Kalachakra mandala would be destroyed. That was an unforgettable day. We returned to camp different persons compared to when we had climbed to the Monastery that morning. We had a sense of gratitude and joy spread in all our being and particularly within our hearts.

CHAPTER 5

EXPERIENCES WITH THE ENTITIES

I do not know if the angels have wings and are as beautiful as we imagine them, what I know for certain is that I have near to me (and I am convinced that we all have near us) an entity that sometimes communicates with me in various ways. Statistically, I've noticed that it happens, both to me and to other people I know, when we are alone. I am not able to formulate an opinion on this fact, much less try to explain. The only thing I can say is that it seems that the presence of other people somehow disturbs this flow of communication.

During the ten years that I was alone after the divorce several episodes happened to me, some even after my second marriage. Let's go in chronological order. In those years I traveled a lot for work and I used to throw myself across the bed to rest even if for just five or ten minutes at any time of day. That particular day I had an important business meeting and I had gone home to get changed and then go to the meeting. After the shower I put on my underwear, but I wanted to rest a few minutes before getting dressed. So I lay across the bed and, without meaning to, fell asleep. At one point I felt something hard on my back at shoulder height, and I felt poked twice. Then I had a strong feeling of being supported by something very hard, maybe a hard briefcase or handbag, and I was convinced of this while, annoyed, I woke up. I thought I had been stupid to have left a bag on the bed right where I had lain down to have a nap. Then I tried to get hold of the bag with my hand and move it. Failing to grab anything behind my shoulder, I got up to look better. After sitting up and looking around me with astonishment I realized that there was absolutely nothing on the bed. The feeling of that push, that almost pointed object pressing against the back of my shoulder was still very strong, I knew I had not imagined it. I was awakened on purpose, by whom? Or by what? I was very grateful in any case because this way I had time to get dressed and arrive on time to the meeting, so important to my job. I knew that I could not have "imagined" what had just happened, I had woken up because I had been poked several times, even while half asleep because I did not want to get up.

At Conventions, respectively in Stockholm and Paris between 1991 and 1995

The following winter I had to catch a plane at 7:30 in the morning from Malpensa airport in Milan, at that time I lived in the Lodi area. My job, as Public Relations and Congress Manager, was to be at the Convention site two days before it started in order to set up the company's stand and control our room reservations for our guests. The alarm was set at 4:30 am. When it rang I had every intention of getting up, but it was very cold and I decided to stay in bed only another five minutes. I fell asleep again. At some point I feel surrounded by a wonderful warmth and love, while a sweet voice was calling me by name. I replied, "yes, tell me" and the voice continued, "Carmen it's time to get up. Get up or you will lose the plane." I replied again, and the voice repeated continuously until I finally got up and went to the bathroom and while I showered I continued my conversation. At a certain point, I wondered who on earth I was talking to? I could have thought I was just talking to myself if it was not for that strong feeling of love that had surrounded me and the strong and clear memory of that voice, so loud and clear, after I was wide awake. I kept that tone of voice with me on the way up to the Malpensa airport and as I drove in the middle of the blizzard I remembered very well the sound of that voice and the love that had surrounded me. I was filled with a sense of gratitude and joy. I tried during the entire journey to the airport to decide if it was a male or female voice but it was very difficult to say, it seemed a little of one and some of the other, perhaps neutral!

DAKAR 2001

It happened that a member of my Rotary Club was invited to speak at a Convention on the environment held in Dakar. He was unable to attend because of previous engagements, so I was asked to make a presentation in his place. It was since 1991 that I went very regularly to Senegal first, to schedule a medical Convention and then for humanitarian aid purposes. At first this was a private initiative and then after the 2001 Convention on the Environment, it was continued through the Rotary Club. The Convention went very well and my presentation on the possible actions to be taken in order to fight desertification, from a Rotarian point of view, aroused much interest. Of course I read the Power Point presentation prepared by the Rotarian originally invited, but which talked about my projects already carried out and with which I was very familiar.

My speech at the Convention on stopping the Desertification, South of the Sahara, held in Dakar in 2001.

At the end of the Convention, the President of the Republic of Senegal, Abdulai Wade, invited all the foreign delegation to the Presidential Palace for a collective meeting with him personally. I was very excited and happy, the presentation went very well and now this unexpected meeting with Abdulai Wade. The President turned out to be a very available and polite person and he asked questions to each one of us. I still have the picture that the President took with all of us in the main hall of the Palace.

After the Convention I went to Sally on the coast, an hour and a half south of Dakar, for a week to rest a little as I had done for many years. Whenever my job became too stressful and I needed to spend some time alone to recharge, I would take a flight to Dakar. The resorts in Sally are well equipped for tourism and very enjoyable and I found myself with my pleasant solitude that allowed me to think a lot, both about the latest events and about my life in general. I had breakfast, as well as all the other meals, always alone, I went to the beach to read and sunbathed alone, I was not looking for the company of anyone, quite happy to enjoy my own.

After three days a blond Italian lady approached me, and asked if she could join me. Even if I really wanted to be alone, somehow, I could not refuse. So we kept each other company in the following days and she told me she was a flight attendant for Alitalia on long distances and had been able to exceptionally take those few days of vacation without her husband and her son. She slowly opened her eyes to the magic of Senegal and the Senegalese people. She was a beautiful woman, and of course there was more than one Senegalese who was courting her, but one in particular she liked very much. I urged her to open up to this new experience, especially considering that she was unhappy in her marriage relationship and carried on only because she had no alternatives. At first she resisted but then soon discovered the infinite sweetness of giving and receiving in a pure way, with no second ends, without conditions of any kind. She experienced an exchange of love not polluted by anything external. A week after my return to Italy I received a postcard from her saying, "I'm sitting outside, in the Fifth Avenue in New York, it's snowing and everything is more beautiful and amazing than ever before. Everything is wonderful, if I think that only yesterday I was in the heat of Senegal where I experienced a magic spell that makes me see everything in a new magical light, it seems impossible. That experience has changed my life and I thank you heartily for this. I will always remember you and thank you for what you have given me and for what we have shared."

During those days when she was meeting with her love in Sally, I had a "problem" to be solved. One night while we went to dinner, my hostess friend and I, we stumbled across one of the Hotel animators. We literally stumbled in the sense that he physically came on to me on purpose! He was a young man much taller than I and really very handsome and when he greeted me he almost made me fall over. It was, according to him, the only way for him to be noticed by me. He invited himself to our table for dinner and told me that all the women, especially the French, were always wanting to make "friends" with him with the specific purpose of taking him to their bed. But I was different and did not even look at him, I went alone to the beach and I sat alone for days, I never even tried to look for company. In actual fact I had noticed him, he was so tall and handsome that it was really impossible not to, but my interest in him finished there. The thing that struck me and that perhaps explains his strong attraction for me was when he told me that when I gave him my hand, the first time, and every time he took my hand after that, a light passed through his arm and went straight to his heart. That meant that he felt my Reiki. He was a man, or rather a boy (although of major age) who was particularly sensitive and captured my Reiki light more than most people. The problem was that I had no intention, even though I was a single woman, of having a young lover, neither Senegalese nor other. Instead he was almost in despair because I did not take seriously his feelings, I did not believe him. He told me that he had put his heart at my feet and I did not believe him, he told me that I did not understand the importance of this fact. He was so sincere and insistent that I began to really worry. When a young person falls in love, or believes to be in love, he can act crazy or make crazy gestures. I could not get him to understand that I did not have the same feelings for him, that I think love has to be on both sides. It was useless, he kept saying he did not want a relationship of only sex, that he wanted to be my man, that he wanted a commitment and so on. Days went by and the date of my departure came nearer. Two days before he informed me that he was going to Dakar to see his mother (to whom he had already spoken about me). That night he was desperate, he could not leave me without obtaining a promise from me to keep in touch, he wanted at all costs my phone number and e-mail address, which I had no intention of giving him. Instead I told him once and for all that it was not possible, but to show him that I did believe that his feelings were real, I took off my gold chain with a medal of Hanuman that I had purchased in Hanpi in India after returning from the leper colony, and gave it to him. I explained where it came from and that Hanuman is the Indian Deity of courage and healing, which would help him heal from that love and which would give him courage in his life. He was very moved by this gesture and seemed to accept that our relationship would have to end there. Finally.

When I woke up the next day I wondered if I had done the right thing by giving him that medal which was, for me, so precious. He went to Dakar and I spent the entire day relaxing.

That night I went to bed wondering what was the meaning of the meeting with this young man, and above all, what was the meaning of my participation at the Convention on the environment. I had really felt like a fish out of water, they were all experts in the environment, so what was I doing in their midst?

In the morning I woke up with the presence of two Entities next to me, one at my feet and one on my left side near my shoulder. I felt enveloped by the now familiar wonderful warmth of love and I was told that my purpose there was to plant trees, to help stop the advancing of the desert, this was one of the purposes of my karma. As I got up and went to the bathroom I replied that now I understood a little better my presence on occasion of the Convention in Senegal. It was at that moment that I realized in full their presence, their whispering. I was amazed at the strength of their presence, I was amazed at how much they had been clear with me and how I could not equivocate on their presence. I whispered a thanks which came from the deepest part of me, while I continued my morning ritual with a sense of gratitude that I knew so well.

Ziano Piacentino 2005

We had agreed to make a Reiki exchange after dinner at the home of my dear friend Palmyra. The house was a great nineteenth century villa on the edge of a small village overlooking the countryside of Piacenza / Pavia surrounded by a large park. Restored by her parents, who had died some years before, it was a home that exuded love and attention to detail, arranged with very good taste and was practical and livable without losing any of its historic atmosphere.

We settled on the great hall on the upper floor, leading to the bedrooms, to the wardrobe and the large bathrooms. In this large hall, furnished like a sitting area, we settled on the floor on a large oriental rug. There were four of us, three of my students and myself. I was treating Palmyra and one of my friends was giving Reiki to the other student. I applied the symbols as usual and while I had "hands on" doing Reiki, with my eyes closed, I began to feel a certain emotion, the tears began to fall, without a reason. After a few minutes they arrived, over my shoulders, two "Entities". They went around and stood in front of me on the other side of Palmyra, who was always lying on the ground, on her back with her eyes closed too.

I could see them perfectly even though I had my eyes closed, in a "blue print", that is, as if they were negative. Two elongated shapes of which I could distinguish well their heads, shoulders and part of the body that ended in a form only very slightly distinguishable. Palmira's parents had died a few years before from a serious illness at a short distance from each other and now they were there, in front of me.

I felt enveloped in an embrace of love, I finally felt understood. So I freed myself of all my pain for the love story that had been cut short unfairly and especially badly by my lover. Knowing that I would be understood by them, knowing they would have compassion I allowed the tears to flow freely and I felt them close to me. Their message was "he does not love you, he has never loved you. He does not deserve all the love that you give him" And I replied," I knew deep down, I should have known right away instead of investing so much." I could not stop the strong flow of tears. I had started my catharsis. It was already a few years that I was "single" and maybe I wanted that relationship with that person because I thought he was the one that would have accompanied me in my old age, but I was completely wrong! I did not know then that the right one would arrive a few years later!

The remarkable thing about all this was the conversation that took place with them, it was <u>not</u> verbally <u>but with the heart</u> more than the mind, telepathically. It was a truly amazing experience. One of the most amazing I have ever had. Communication between Souls, between three Souls, one of which still incarnated.

They stood there a little longer and then disappeared. I tried unsuccessfully to control my tears and my friend doing the other treatment could not help but notice. But he said nothing and did not ask me anything. Then Palmyra noticed how upset I was and told me to stay a little longer after all the others had left. So I did and I told her what had happened. She was not surprised at all and was very glad that somehow her parents had come to give me advice, to comfort me. It's strange that Palmyra had asked me for help, she had asked for a Reiki treatment because she was very tired and a bit depressed and in actual fact it was me who needed help and did not know who to ask for it. In the end it was her who, through her parents, had helped me!

My need for love had made me blind to the obvious truth, and it was therefore a true gift the appearance of those two Souls so affectionate and full of love. They were able to read the very bottom of my heart. We were at the beginning of August, I was at home alone and on vacation, so for the first time since that famous time in England when an "Entity" had saved my life at the age of eighteen, I could now again cry at will. So I continued my catharsis which had begun that night at the home of Palmyra. I cried until physically ill for two days and two nights. Then my friend Palmyra invited me back to her big house in the country to recover a bit. She asked me where I wanted to sleep, I could choose between the free room next to her on the first floor or in the attic where there was an apartment available. I chose the room on the first floor, which was where her father had died and in which no one had slept in since then. I was happy to sleep in that room, I seemed to feel a bit of the warmth that I had experienced that famous night we did Reiki in the upstairs hall and I had met her parents. It was a large and beautiful room with a vaulted ceiling with refined paintings of flowers. The walls of the room were painted red. I lit a candle and some incense and made my usual meditation before going to bed that night, when I went upstairs after dinner. Early in the morning, no longer in a deep sleep, but not yet awake, I was thinking about my pain and suffering, about the way I had been deceived. Suddenly I felt enveloped by the warmth I had already known and I felt the understanding and infinite love already experienced that famous evening. Palmira's Father said, "that's right, he does not love you, you must not fool yourself any further. You'll find the right one for you, do not worry." That warmth and those words comforted me greatly, and I was amazed to experience once again the dialogue with a disembodied Soul, that clear non verbal communication of the heart.

I have asked myself many times since then if that is the common method of communication between all Souls when they are no longer in the material world. My heart fills with gratitude for this extraordinary experience every time my mind goes back to my encounter with those loving Souls.

A Rotary Club evening during my year of presidency in which we hosted little Marie and her mother. Marie was treated at the San Matteo hospital in Pavia, funded by our Club for a tuberculosis of the bones, which healed completely.

Malpensa Airport in 2001

I had not seen my Old Master for several years so it was a nice surprise to meet him that day at Malpensa airport. I had accompanied my brother and sister in law who were going back to Madrid and he had accompanied a beautiful girl who was probably Indian and her expressions of despair made it very clear that she had to depart without him, probably for London or India. She did not want to leave him and was almost in tears, he instead was almost irritated by her "pantomime" in the sense that they must have already cleared between them how things stood, long before arriving at the airport. That attachment and non-acceptance of the fact that she had to leave was clearly bothering him. We exchanged a quick "hello" then he ran with her into the terminal. I said goodbye to my relatives and I went back to my car. While leaving the departure area of the airport all of a sudden I was seized with an explosion of total and deep joy, completely irrational and unreasonable. I could not understand why on earth I was so happy to see him. It had been years since we last saw each other and we were no longer in touch. It was true that he was a very handsome man, but I knew many very handsome men who caused me no emotions whatsoever. I had no relationship with him except that of Master-pupil friendship, which had not been cultivated for several years. I had perhaps never experienced a joy so strong . As I drove my mind tried to find a rational foothold to explain that feeling so excessively strong and I ended up concluding that it could not be a feeling that belonged to this life. It was a feeling of my Soul in relation to something belonging to my past lives. Perhaps what I had "lived" in my regression and what had also been seen by a Psychic was true, maybe he really had been my teacher and lover in ancient Greece. My Soul rejoiced so much for that brief encounter, well beyond my rational mind and my feelings in this life, to make it feasible. It was as if there was another me who rejoiced for something that almost didn't concern me. But I felt the joy physically too, it was as if there were two Carmens. A really weird feeling. A feeling that was mine but did not belong to anything in my life today.

The ancient life we had lived together was the only explanation, it gave a logical and acceptable sense to such an extraordinary, irrational and otherwise inexplicable experience.

A few days later I received an email from him in which he apologized for having greeted me so hastily, but he had hoped to see me when he came back out to greet me properly. Unfortunately I had already left

2006

To conclude my stories regarding psychics, although I find it rather odd, it is perhaps only a natural and logical sequence considering the above, that it was a psychic that "forced" me to go back to my current Reiki Master, by giving me a message for him. After ten years that we did not hear from each other nor had we seen each other, I traced him through his web site and asked to meet him because I had to deliver a message received by a Psychic and addressed to him. At first he welcomed me very well on the phone, then like the good Master that he is, he wanted to close old issues, old circles still open, that he had with me and that were still pending. He asked me to explain why I had "turned my back on him" ten years before, taking me completely by surprise. I found it hard there and then to give a plausible explanation, but he kept asking me questions until he dug out the real reasons, the aspects which I had not considered. We made an appointment to meet the following week, but in the meantime, right after that call, I was very ill for about three days. I reviewed in my mind all the events of my Reiki experience with the Master, I went over the real reason why I had left, and of course it also became very clear the real reason why I had had to return.

What can I say, thank goodness that we receive such help every now and then, at least from my point of view. Probably persons less stubborn and less hard headed than I am do not need this kind of help and in some ways can even do without it. I can only say I am thankful and grateful for all the help that I receive that allows me to get back on my karmic path. This kind of help that will allow me to put in practice my task in this life. It seems clear that you cannot escape from your karma. I've been avoiding it for ten years, now I realize that I have to start working seriously on my task, whether I like it or not. Probably the message that I gave to my Master has not even been considered, he being very wise and a true Master, he knew immediately that that message was only an instrument to make me go back home. In fact, during that famous long phone call he asked me nothing about the message from the Psychic. instead he came out with everything that he had withheld during those ten years, asking me questions which literally put me with my back to the wall.

The realization that I had to start organizing Reiki courses, that I could not keep putting it off any longer, grew stronger and stronger. For this reason I decided to face my demons and to allow my chakras to be treated by the only person who I would allow to touch them. Apparently our chakras, as well as all the most popular features, also preserve the memories of the past lives of our Soul. Part of these memories can be revealed only when our Soul had decided, before incarnating, that this should happen. It does not happen to everyone simply because not everyone needs to take a look at their past lives. Apparently it only happens if there is a specific reason. For example, if that Soul needs to close emotional "circles" still pending or any other issue usually somehow connected with the present life, being the present life an opportunity for resolution.

CHAPTER 6

My friend Elisa has, for many years, attended the course of a person who, together with her husband had done a lot of astral travelling. Together, they had visited the ancient population of the Essenes from whom they had learned and later taught others, the Essen healing treatments. Elisa is in any case a very gifted person of her own, independently from this ancient healing method. I never allow anyone to touch my chakras except her, especially considering what happens to me when she treats them. Ten years ago I had my first Essene treatment with Elisa and when she placed her hand on the second chakra I felt a strange pain that began to rise up to the Fifth Chakra, where I began to talk about what I "saw".

In actual fact, also what I "felt" because I was overcome by a strong and terrible fear, because there were people putting me on a pile of wood to burn me alive !! This is how I made my first regression to a past life. Only the awakened and those with an open mind can understand, especially if they have experienced a regression themselves. For all you others, I realize and understand that it is very difficult to accept this fact.

MEDEIVAL PERIOD- THE INQUISITION

All those soldiers, they arrived in dozens at a time, taken in wagons to a field hospital, where, with the very few resources available to her, she tried to do something, the best she could, to relieve their pain and to assist them in their last hour. All of them, and some were very young, tried to attract the attention and help of that lady who was dressed pretty finely, definitely not a nurse, but who turned to the wounded with so much calmness and who was illuminated with a strange light, naturally attracting their attention. She would hold out her hand and place it on a wound and it would close, as if pasted by an invisible glue. Their pain stopped immediately and the soldiers, amazed and grateful, barely managed to whisper a thank you, with their eyes full of love and wonder towards that person so special. On her part, she moved amongst them and chose with great difficulty where to put her hands first, the soldiers were so many and so badly wounded. The doctor pretended not to see what was going on. The nurses on the other hand, with great astonishment and admiration, indicated to her the most severe cases, where to stop the bleeding first, where to lay her hands to allow a soldier to breathe again despite his crushed lungs, and so on. This happened throughout the entire day and for all the following days and for many months after.

The sounds in the backyard were more boisterous than usual when she woke up that morning to the voice of a woman who was screaming her name. She asked her to do something for the baby that she carried in her arms, lifeless. She was followed by a bevy of other women who were trying to console the mother, the voices echoing in the small courtyard. Now there was nothing left to do for the child. But the mother did not want to give up, and so had come, full of hope, to look for the woman with special powers, who nursed and healed the soldiers. She took the little baby and, whilst bringing it towards her breathed gently but firmly on the child's head, on the so called "fountain". A few seconds later the child awoke, as if from a long sleep and started crying. There was a murmured mixture of awe and fear from all the witnesses of this "work of the devil". It was the first time she heard those words. Unfortunately, it would not be the last. A few days later the scene was repeated, this time it was a very young mother, her child was probably stillborn. She did the same, and once again the same extraordinary awakening of the little child occurred. The baby began to cry a few minutes after she had blown on its head. By now everyone was talking about what had happened and while some looked at her with surprise and admiration, others were almost annoyed by these successes. These unexplained and unusual skills caused some people to look at her with suspicion, if not with hatred. When they brought the third child the healer was almost a little afraid to make the same gestures, she feared the consequences because she had heard strange voices and strange comments. Many people believed that she was possessed by a super natural force, others that it was all the work of the devil. In any case, she could not withdraw from answering the request of the third mother, who was in total despair. She had turned to her for help, and to tell the truth even when she was specifically asked to bring the woman's daughter back to life the healer didn't really know exactly what happened. Every time she blew on the head of those babies, they came back to life. She didn't know how, but she did know that it worked and that in any case she did nothing wrong, to the contrary, she did much good.

Unfortunately, not everyone thought like that, many were convinced that she was possessed and one day they arrived in the small courtyard of her house. Six men in uniform that morning knocked loudly with arrogance on her door and without an explanation of any kind, dragged her away. She was very agitated and worried, she could not free herself from their grip and she knew that nothing good was waiting for her. Indeed, deep down she knew she was going towards a terrible fate. They put her in the wooden wagon with the borders almost up to her shoulders, along with other women, some of whom she knew by sight. The wagon was pulled by a horse and was driven into a large square. There where already a large number of people that gathered to watch. As the wagon made its way through the crowd the people were shouting all kinds of insults at all the women therein. She was almost numb with fear and did not hear anything, not even a sound, everything was muffled. However, she could see their faces, all very angry, as if they had a personal issue to settle with her. She could feel their hatred towards her person for some imagined terrible crime, which she had definitely never committed. People she had never seen before. Her hearing somehow returned when they stopped the wagon and invited her to descend. She found herself in front of a long table with four people dressed in black with a white collar and black hair who were watching her very carefully and strictly. The Holy Inquisition! They called her by name and she nodded in reply, she was not able to do anything else for she was too caught up and in terror of what clearly was waiting for her. She could not take her eyes off the various stacks of wood prepared at a certain distance from them. The inquisitors kept talking and the crowd continued to scream, but she could not hear anything. When they dragged her to one of those piles she started screaming with all her might. She was overcome by terror and could not do anything to break free. They tied her hands to the pole in the middle of the pile of wood, after dragging her up it, then they tied her feet. At that point they set fire to the stack. Suddenly she stopped screaming, perhaps because she was stricken by a sense of great injustice. Why were they doing this when she only did good? She was not a witch, she was not the daughter of the devil, she was not against the church. She did have some unexplained powers, but was that her fault? She thought, or rather she had convinced herself, that those looks of gratitude of hundreds of soldiers that she had healed would have somehow protected her from this madness. Admittedly to resurrect three babies was something strong and extraordinary, she could not explain what had happened or why, but what is certain is that she had made no "agreement" with anyone! It just happened and that's it. How could it be explained ?

She began coughing because of the smoke that began seeping into her nostrils and lungs.

Elisa brought me back whilst I was still coughing and had the strong smell of smoke in my nostrils. I began to think that maybe this was the reason why I coughed a lot every time someone lit a cigarette in my presence. But the most important question was: why had I been allowed to regress into a past life?

The second time, during my therapy with Elisa, the scene developed further.

———— ᴠᴠᴠᴑᴄᴎᴄᴛᴎᴄᴛᴎᴄᴑᴠᴠᴠ ————

When the smoke almost choked the healer, a man of the law, in a loud voice, so as to be heard over the screams of the crowd, turned to the bench of the Inquisitors and explained everything that the woman had done. She had gone to the field hospitals, for the sake of their soldiers that had returned from the war front with serious injuries, almost dead, to heal them as best as she could, by simply laying her hands on their wounds. It was a natural gift, a gift of God, and certainly not the work of evil. The inquisitors then asked what he had to say about the three infants that had been resuscitated, how was he going to explain that devilry. The man of law insisted that it was also a gesture of goodness They should consider that. While other women were accused of "witchery" and sorcery and were blamed for giving potions for various purposes, this woman had saved three little babies, had done only a good deed. In the end, only due to their admiration for the man of law, and perhaps also in order not to go against the power that he had over the people, they decided to make an exception and bring the healer down from the stake. But only on one condition, she had to be precluded from the possibility of continuing with her practices.

At one point the man of the law heard an almost inhuman scream, which was by far louder than the deafening noise of the crowd. He looked almost with fear towards the group of women gathered around the person screaming, he came up to them, and they let him pass, with a strange expression on their faces. When he got to the woman who had just been taken down from the stake, she had her back turned. He realized that it was her screaming just then, he felt scared by the smell he could perceive, but turned her towards him and almost threw up. The poor woman was all disfigured, her mouth was almost all gone, her cheeks were all wrinkled and black, he could not believe his eyes! They had put a lit ember of wood in her mouth so she could no longer practice the "breath of life".

It was not enough, now two soldiers took her and dragged her to where there was a blacksmith nearby, they forced her to keep her hands on the burning fire until all her flesh was burned and they could see the bones of her fingers, Again he heard the screams and the man of law, with a heavy heart for such cruelty had to turn away, unable to watch the scene. It was bad enough to hear her scream, now almost like that of an animal.

───────⟋⟍∘⟍∘⟋∘⟍∘───────

Elisa, to bring me back, once the torturers had finished with me, made me look at my hands and then look to one side where there was a pond, she made me go there, and put my hands in the water. Once they had cooled I started feeling a little better, the physical pain began passing. Gradually Elisa's voice led me back. During that Essen therapy session I not only felt all the pain and suffering that I had endured in that life, but also the smell of my burning flesh. For years after that experience I have not been able to eat grilled meat and for a very long time the simple idea of meat on a grill and the mere smell made me feel very ill.

If it was all a fantasy, can the imagination can go that far?

Anecdote: One of the inquisitors had the same face of an ex colleague of mine today. That inquisitor has paid her debt too, by the law of cause and effect. Without my knowing, without my least suspecting, my female colleague and friend, who had the same face as one of the inquisitors was in love with me. However I never had any feelings of that kind for any female and certainly not for her. Therefore she never received any response from my part. In the ten years that I had been first separated and then divorced, I wondered how many "films" in her mind's eye, she had made up on the two of us. Who knows how many illusions and dis-illusions she went through. Unfortunately, her wishful castle collapsed with the arrival of Edward, my second husband. One day without any notice, she completely cut off all communications. I could not talk to her or obtain answers via e-mail, etc. After much insistence on my part I received two lines where she explained that she hoped one day to be able to explain to me but at the moment it was impossible. Only then did I finally begin to realize what had been going on. It was then that I began to put together all the pieces of the past few years. Sometimes it is true that we do not see what is obvious and right under our nose because it is too far away from what we are, from our real nature. In a way I felt very sorry for her but on the other hand I was angry at her for "abandoning" me in such a way after so many years of friendship, that I had valued as such.

I love Venice, like millions of other people, so I never thought it would be a "deja vu" as a result of a life spent there. I have always felt very much at home, in an inexplicable and profound way. I felt a deep happiness while wandering the streets among all those beautiful colors of the works and glass of Murano I always liked it so very deeply and so very very much, it is only now that I understand a little better that deep and inner feeling and inner voice.

VENICE 1725

She was walking happily in the streets enjoying the beautiful sunny day and the fact that soon she would see the one person that made her heart beat so crazily. In many greeted her as she walked passed them in her new aquamarine brocade dress, with her hair tied at the back of her head but loose on her shoulders, her fresh sixteen year old face, with the smile of someone who believed that life had in store great joys for her. While crossing the fruit and vegetable market on the Grand Canal she said hello to several people who knew her since she was a baby. Then she saw him, tall and blond with curly hair and a sweet face who looked like an angel, leaning against a wall he was waiting for her to walk by. She gave him a long smile while her eyes sparkled with joy. He literally took her all in, as he smiled back, following her with his eyes until she disappeared around the corner at the end of the market. She could not see him again until the next market day which was the following week, her mother would not have allowed her to go out alone until that time. She met with her mother, who was waiting for her down the alley. Her mother was wearing a stern expression and her favorite red satin dress. Her mother informed her that that would be the last time she allowed her to go out alone because she had been betrothed and was to marry one of the most important noblemen of Venice. This meant that the young girl had to be prepared for the wedding by being practically held in seclusion. She protested and told her mother that she did not even know him, let alone love him. The nobleman was in any case too old and she wanted to marry someone else. Her mother told her to forget all that nonsense because she had already given her word. It would be a great marriage because the young girl would have ensured a future of ease and wealth, not only for herself but also for her mother.

When a few weeks later her mother organized their first official meeting, she was very nervous and depressed. However, when she saw him she was quite surprised, not so much for the fact that he looked younger than she expected, but because she knew him. Her mind went to the many times she had seen him in the past with her mother. Suddenly she realized why she knew him. They had been lovers. How could her mother have done such a thing to her? How could she protest? There seemed no way out for the young girl, she had to accept. On the day of her marriage, she remembered very little of that event which was so important to the Society of Venice. Married life, to her surprise, turned out to be not as bad as she had thought. Her noble husband was very helpful and very patient with her. The wedding was in fact consumed several weeks later. He had had the patience to wait for when she was ready and only then very gently made a woman of her, made her his wife.

Donna Rachele was happy. She had reached her goal, even though her lover had not wanted to marry her. According to the Noble Venetian, Donna Rachele was not suited to the role of wife of such a noble person as himself, who was so important and well known. However, when she proposed her daughter as a bride, he could not resist. The idea of having such a pretty young bride as was her daughter, and be able to also continue to keep his mistress was very appealing.. It seemed really an ideal situation also to Donna Rachele. She had been very happy to make up for the absence of her daughter in his bed. For her it was the ideal situation, she wished it to continue like that forever. The marriage of her daughter had secured a place in Society as the mother-in-law of the nobleman and mother of the bride. No one seemed to remember her as a merry widow any more. She had guaranteed herself a wonderful home, the ground floor of the palace on the Grand Canal, the nobleman and the continuation of their love. Everything was perfect.

With each passing month, however, the nobleman began to fall in love with his young wife, and felt less and less pleasure during his meetings with Donna Rachele. As time went by he began to thin out the meetings with her more and more, up to almost avoid meeting her altogether. At first by giving her a thousand excuses, later he did not even bother to give her any explanation at all. This angered Donna Rachele a lot and it took her very little to understand the real reason for this continuous postponing of their rendezvous. She was furious, she would not lose her lover and wanted to avenge the humiliation of the rejection. Mindful of the old feelings that her daughter had for that handsome young man with curly hair and clear blue eyes, she decided to enact her revenge. A plan that would have taken away her opponent, even if it was her daughter, and would have left the way clear for her to continue her relationship with her lover. She would be the one to comfort him, she would be the one take care of her nobleman.

So she reported to the Venetian Sire that his young wife was cheating on him with a young Venetian, curly-haired, well-born young man who was the former love of her wife, never forgotten. At first the nobleman did not believe it, but Donna Rachele insisted so much, that doubt began to creep in. Therefore now, every time his wife wanted to go out on her own, Donna Rachele made him notice it. Every time she looked a little 'thoughtful, Donna Rachele pointed it out. Finally she offered to follow her daughter personally and then report back to the Nobleman. It was so easy for Donna Rachele to invent the meeting of the bride with her young lover. When she reported in detail the meeting of the bride with her lover, how he had embraced her, how he had kissed her, where they had gone, which "calle paths" they had strolled in, hand in hand, which Inn they had stopped and what they had done, the Nobleman was blinded by a furious jealousy. He was so furious that he had lost his mind, unable to even consider the possibility of verifying what had been reported by Donna Rachele, blindly trusting his mistress. He waited in an altered state of mind that his bride come down for dinner and then tackled her immediately. He accused her very strongly and badly and continued asking Donna Rachele, (who nodded every time) confirmation to what he was saying.

The young girl could only defend herself by denying. Unfortunately, her husband did not believe her, he was completely blinded by his jealousy. The bride looked absolutely incredulous at her mother, she could not believe that her own mother had betrayed her twice, first her mother had forced her to marry a man she did not love, who was much older than her, and then she had invented this story to get her out of the way. How was it possible? How could she be so cruel and manipulative with her own flesh and blood?

The Nobleman grabbed his young bride by the arm and took her to the top floor of the "palazzo" or building, in a room for guests, and while dragging her all the way up the stairs ordered Donna Rachele to call the mason and have him come immediately up with bricks and mortar.

The young bride was terrified, crying in despair, she could not believe what was happening. When they arrived on the top floor the Nobleman would not let go of his bride's arm until the mason arrived, followed by Donna Rachele. He brought his young bride to the end of the room and pushed her against the wall behind the bed, moving it three-quarters out of the way and ordered the builder to start laying bricks thirty, forty inches in front of her. The Mason was shocked and looked for a moment at the Nobleman to make sure he had understood. When the latter told him to hurry up, he still couldn't believe his ears. So it was that, with a very heavy heart, the Mason began putting one brick next to each other then one on top of the other, soon building a wall.

The bride, inside the wall, was now leaning against the wall, the Nobleman held her arm until the wall was too high for her to climb over. Crying in despair she kept asking and begging her husband to have mercy, she repeated that she had done nothing to deserve such a terrible end. But both the Nobleman and her mother were standing there, indifferent to her tears and her supplications. He was still blinded by his furious anger and jealousy and she was glad to be rid of her rival. Soon, the Mason had to climb a ladder and put the last bricks, himself crying too. He was torn by the tears and entreaties of the young bride.

In the dark, alone with her despair, the bride at the beginning pounded her fists on the wall but could not bring it down. The bricks were very large, and perhaps the Mason had put a reinforcement on the other side, making her efforts futile. Then she began to lack oxygen, she felt suffocated, the lack of air made her panic. She coughed continuously due to the cement dust that caught her throat.

At one point, several hours later, maybe the next day, she began to stop crying. She knew it was useless, she realized she was dying, her short life would end there. With the clarity that comes to mind in those moments, she sent a deep and heartfelt curse to Donna Rachele, "I curse you mother, you'll pay for this, for all the terrible things you have done to me, you will pay very badly, I curse you to pay very bitterly and very heavily, I curse you … ". Those were her last thoughts.

─────❀❀❀─────

I returned from that regression with a strong flavor of fresh concrete in my mouth!

I ask you: can one's imagination lead to a real and concrete physical flavor in your mouth? Or is this the proof that there was actually a regression in time, not only of memory but also of the Soul? Can imagination cause such strong feelings of fear and terror, can imagination make you cry as it happens in dreams, even if you are awake but with your eyes closed? During these therapies I was awake, I felt transported to another time and space. I felt all the excitement of what was happening in every part of me, but still I heard the voice of my therapist.

In the first regression in that life, I stopped at the time when the Mason put the last brick. I was screaming and crying not only in memory, but physically in today's reality,

I felt as if I was simultaneously in 1725 and in 2000, I felt so real the fear, the terror and the tears did come flowing down my face as a carbon copy of what I was experiencing in 1725!! The Essen therapist helped me come back from the regression. She made me look at my hands, then gave me the following instructions: with your hands remove one brick at a time and create a big hole in the wall, then get out of there and go outside, take a deep breath, you're safe there, you're safe now.

The second time I made the regression to that life it was easier to come back because I was a little quieter, I was no longer screaming. I had found myself at the end when I was dying and I had cursed my then mother. The curse that, apparently, that Soul has paid in this century. I met her in this life, my "mother" of that time. Elisa knew already when I went to her the first time ten years ago but she did not tell me., She already channeled every time she was expecting a person for treatment. In fact, when she learned that I was going with a friend that I saw regularly (we belonged to a small group of people who gathered while another friend of ours, who channeled an important text very good for the evolution of Mankind!) she dissuaded me. With many excuses she convinced me to go with someone else. Which I did. In fact, I went with a lawyer friend who acted as a witness to my regressions. My mother of that time, in this life is in turn tormented by her Venetian Noble mother. Even in this life, her actual mother has ruined her existence, so much so that she split up with her husband. Her mother tormented her to the point that she wanted to commit suicide. This sent her into a strong depression from which she struggled a lot to come out of.

ANCIENT GREECE - YEAR 3000 BC

The great priestess of the temple that day was restless, she had a bad feeling, She knew that something bad would happen even if she could not identify for sure exactly what. The usual crowd of people huddled just outside the temple waiting for her to show herself and perform her rituals. She was very popular and loved by the people who more and more participated to the propitiatory rituals of their culture and participated even more closely to the healing rituals of well-being given by the High Priestess. She was the woman, or rather the person, who was the most powerful of all the Ancient Greek City. She prepared herself as usual, with personal purifying ablutions ritual and had then sprinkled incense and perfumes all over her body. Her maids helped her dress, first with the long, flowing linen dress in direct contact with her skin, then over this, another much lighter dress, with a white and purple sash at the waist that completed the whole outfit. Her long brown hair was loose down her back but tied back with a braid intersected by a purple thread circling her head and held at the neck. All this time she recited something in a low voice so her maids could not hear the sacred words while, constantly holding two snakes, one in either hand.

Everything happened under the watchful eye of her Master, who had taught her everything. He protected and warmed her heart, and also took care of the real woman behind the Priestess, in addition to the technical teachings. He had brought her up in the temple since she was a little child. As soon as she became a woman, he taught her to perform the ritual of the fertilization of Mother Earth, in order to obtain a good harvest for the whole nation. During the spring solstice, the young Priestess was prepared with the special rituals during the night and at dawn, followed by the entire population, she went into the fields. There, at one point when she had chosen where, she opened her legs widely and two maids pulled up her dress a little, just enough so the people could see with their own eyes the blood of the holy priestess bless the earth. Her sacred blood was then absorbed with an incredible speed and voracity. Meanwhile, arms and face turned upwards towards the Universe, she endlessly recited and dialogued with the Universe itself, for however long she deemed necessary. Finally, as if awakened from a dream, she regained her posture and went back to the temple accompanied by the Master and the assistants and all the people around and behind her. They were all filled with gratitude because they were convinced that the harvest would now be protected from natural disasters and would be abundant. And so it was, year after year.

When she was ready, that day, the Temple assistants opened the grand entrance and she went out. The crowd suddenly fell silent, attentive to her general blessing for all, moving her arms up with the serpents in her hands, forming geometric signs as she addressed the whole crowd. Then the guards allowed a few people at a time to get closer to the stairs where she was waiting to be able to lay her hands on and / or snakes on in order to heal those in need, those who asked for it. Extraordinary healings occurred on those occasions and the population could no longer do without her.

This fact much disturbed the Governors of the Greek City, that Priestess had taken away their power to control the population. They decided to eliminate her and destroy the temple so that she would lose all control over the population and all her traditions would go lost. This is how they hoped to get back their power. She had been there long hours to treat and cure diseases and disorders of her people. She was almost at the end of the long line when she first heard and then saw the soldiers on horseback and on foot. They intruded into the crowd giving the sword to anyone who tried to stop them. They soon came to the gates of the Temple and the great flight of steps where the Priestess was still working. Meanwhile her Master came to her side, a moment before them. The Master of the High Priestess, who fought with great courage until the soldiers surrounded him, they were eight to one, there was no way he could escape, they wounded him to death. They left him there as if he was an ordinary citizen, and charged into the temple. The Priestess was prostrated with grief, she could not believe her eyes, she could not believe that her beloved Master was dead. She was no longer interested in her own life. Her disbelief at what was happening did not allow her to use her powers to defend herself. So when they took her and held her there to witness what they had done to the Temple and to her Master, she was as if in a trance. She did nothing to stop them, without her Master life had no meaning for her. The soldiers set fire where it was possible, and destroyed all the rest, knocking to the ground all the major oil lamps and all the jars of terra cotta containers, full of precious oils, incense and perfumes.

They destroyed everything.

They took the Priestess to a dark prison, dirty and wet, but she was not interested, she did not care anymore. Therefore she took her own life with a surprising calmness. She cut her veins with a sharp knife which she had hidden in her robes when they had dragged her away. She spent the last moments of her short life wondering what was the point in curing all those people, in having all those powers if she could not defend herself nor her people, nor her Master and even less her Temple. She did not know what to make of her powers now, and without her Master, life wasn't worth living, it was better to die. She was found the next day in a pool of blood, lifeless.

———⌇∾⊙⟲⟿⊙⟲⊙⟿∾⌇———

Note: The Master that I knew then I have met again in this life. It's a person I know. The first time I saw him I seemed to read his mind, I captured very well his every change of mood and emotional state. Since then, every time I meet him I am overwhelmed by an irrational deep joy!

Anecdote: Many years before receiving the treatment of the Essenes and therefore before my flash back in Greece, I went for the first time on holiday in Sicily, at Capo Rizzuto, East of Palermo looking at the map. While we were there we decided one day to visit the nearby Segesta Greek Temple. During the trip I was very calm and quiet and very curious because I had not yet been to Greece so it would be my first visit to a ruin of Ancient Greece, but nothing more. Arriving by car you pass by a very wooded area, then suddenly out of nowhere, appears the ancient temple, on a hill, through the trees, therefore you can see it very well at a distance, whilst still approaching it.

My heart did a double jump and I felt a joy so profound that it's really hard to describe. I thought, "maybe everyone feels this deep emotion when one sees for the first time a Greek temple." As we went on and we got closer, I continued to be taken by that strong emotion. What we had seen was only the first part, though perhaps the most important, because then you had to climb the mountain to visit the Greek Theatre and the ruins of the remaining ancient houses.

When we reached the top I was seized with a kind of trance, it was as if I could no longer hear the voices of family and friends, I entered a world of my own. I seemed to be able to imagine very well what had been going on there, like a film. I saw the crowd on the steps used as seats all around and the events going on at the center. It was so emotional that I was almost in tears. I watched with wonder and awe at the mountains all around and the spectacular view of the sea. From there any vessel that approached that part of the Island could be seen very well . I seemed to feel the sense of security that this place gave all the people. I went into the Greek theater with the feeling that I had gone there many times before and I sat in the place of honor, wondering how I knew that there was a place of honor and how I knew exactly where it was. The place felt like there was an air of magic.

Every step gave me powerful and inexplicable emotions, and the place was somehow very familiar.

I attributed all of these emotions to the "magic" of Ancient Greece, I thought that all sensitive people like me would feel the same things, after all that was the basis of all cultures and especially our culture. Therefore, until I went for my Essen treatment with Elisa I thought no more about it.

When I had just finished the treatments and for ten long years afterwards, I had thought that the connection between the past lives and my cough was just a way to make me understand that the cough was due to the terrible experiences in those two lives. In fact whenever I happened to sit next to a person who was smoking, I coughed a lot and I thought I had finally understood why. I thought and hoped that once aware of the reason why I coughed all the time and no one could cure it, with time it would pass. I thought I had been allowed to regress into my past lives so I could use it as a form of treatment, because once aware of the cause, the cough would stop. (In the case of the first two lives). That was not so. My cough continued to remain a mystery, and I still did not understand why I had been allowed to regress into my past lives if the cough did not get any better.

Looking at the experience from a different point of view, I began to think that it had probably happened to me in order that I could close the "circle" so to speak, of the that medieval life. I had been prohibited to continue to help people by having my hands burned burn down to the bone. However, by continuing in this life what had been stopped then, that is "laying hands on" when I do Reiki, I can finally close that circle.

Also during the life as a Priestess in ancient Greece, I was interrupted in my role as a healer, perhaps by doing Reiki, organizing courses, enabling people to do Reiki, I can somehow redeem that interrupted experience. It was stopped so abruptly, but with Reiki,

I am able to execute my 'karmic effect" regarding my life in Ancient Greece.

In the meantime, while I was pursuing my path with Reiki, I met, due to many and various reasons, psychics who have in turn THEY been the ones who have seen some of my other past lives. The reasons why this has happened I cannot yet explain. What is certain is that my past lives "seen" or experienced by those psychics, and not by myself directly, remain almost marginal for me. They do not have the emotional load and strong feelings that are connected with direct flash backs or regressions. Just to complete the picture and as a kind of chronological correctness, I briefly describe the past lives emerged from the psychics that I met during the ten years following my three regressions.

ENGLAND 1600

I was a lawyer, one of the few lives that I was a man, I have almost always been a woman. This lawyer devoted his long life, he lived to be 80 years old which in those days was extraordinary, in the defense of women. Any kind of woman, prostitutes, abused women, women wrongfully accused of anything. He had only women clients. Although he was a very wealthy English lord with a large estate in the country, he never married, his feminine nature was too strong. According to the psychic it was a way for my Soul to compensate the injustice suffered during the Inquisition.

Small anecdote: I usually state that I am English mother tongue because I grew up in England. I often find myself, however, using a very archaic English, unwillingly. Even though I'm in Italy since about forty years I have not totally lost the London / Luton English accent. I don't really notice it much, but other people point it out because they find it quite bizarre! Maybe something emerges from that period?

JAPAN 1500-1700

A famous psychic, during a meditation she saw me very clearly as a Japanese Samurai. It's true that I have a visceral attraction for martial arts, but also do thousands of other people. What is the point of such an event? What escapes my rational mind?

BOSTON - USA 1800

She is a woman, with a botanical passion but her husband will not let me work. She has two children and she spends her life doing research on plants and classifying the various families and groups of wild plants and flowers. She lives to a great age. What sense can this "vision" of my past life in Boston have? It is true that I really like all flowers and plants in general and I have a deep relationship with nature, but so do millions of other people. Therefore, what is the point of this vision? Is it only for me to understand why I am the way I am? It seems too little. There must be a meaning that escapes my understanding. A meaning beyond my reach.

SICILY EARLY 1900

She was a young woman madly in love with a man who had had to leave Sicily because he had to travel, it is unclear whether to immigrate or just to take a trip. The young woman was tormented because her lover asked her to go with him, but she did not want to leave her parents. She feels terribly tied to the land, and does not want to leave her parents, but does not want to lose her beloved either. Eventually he leaves and she stays but she is destroyed by grief. She was not able to go away and now that the end of her life was close she saw no way out. She died young of a broken heart. But before she died, she crossed paths, briefly, without being aware of it, a cardinal, probably the one who had been her teacher in ancient Greece when she was a Priestess.

According to the psychic I have chosen in this incarnation a family without roots to compensate for that terribly binding experience. This strikes me as possible. Let me explain, my great-grandfather emigrated to São Paulo in the late '800 and my grandfather returned to the South of Italy in 1930. At the age of six I was torn from the colorful and fragrant South of Italy to be brought to gray England. At nineteen I left my family, my work and my boyfriend and came back to Italy (even if I did not speak a word of Italian). I have a brother who lives between Madrid, London and New York and another brother who lives in San Francisco since the seventies. I have first cousins in London and Luton and other first cousins in New York. For twenty years I have organized conferences around the world and I have traveled extensively, from New Orleans before the tsunami, to Tokyo and then to all the capitals of Europe, and to Africa where I went regularly for eighteen years in a row and where I organized a Convention with 350 people. Strange huh? Are they just coincidences?

OTHER PERSONAL EXPERIENCES

October 25, 2008, I married Edward, it was my second marriage .

On a material level, love exploded in an irrational and inexplicable way. It was clear to me that it was a Soul attraction. Edward was convinced that because the feeling between us was so strong that there was some sort of upper hand in provoking the meeting. We both knew from the start that we did not want to meet anyone else from the Singles Club. Even though we had not done the registration for only three months but for over a year, we had no interest in getting to know any one else. For some unknown reason, we had found the perfect person for each other. It was a deep feeling, which we were unable to explain, but we were very happy.

ESSEN THERAPY MAY 2010

Elisa, since the old days, before receiving a person for treatment asks for advice to the Entities. On that day I received the message that can be found below. When I arrived she asked me exactly what I feel when I get a cough, what kind of emotion. "I feel suffocated" I replied. She asked when in my life did I feel suffocated. In this life never but in two past lives, yes. So she began to attempt through relaxation and guided meditation, to bring me back to the Middle Ages at the time of the fire. Unfortunately my arm was hurting and this caused me to stop. Elisa said that maybe I was not ready yet, the interruption was an excuse. So she decided to give me a "chakra balancing". I lay on the bed facing upwards and when she put the essential oil on my Second Chakra (I was half-naked) in a leap I found myself back there again. She told me to tell her what I felt and what I saw. I repeated the whole scene again. Then Elisa said, "ask the woman you see at the stake why she is there, why had her / your Soul wanted to make that experience." I did ask and the answer was that I had to pay a debt. Then Elisa made me ask what was the debt. I began to see that there were houses burning and I was there with a torch! I had burned the houses with the people inside, possibly even children. Then I began, led by Elisa, to send light, to send Reiki to forgive myself. Then returning to the scene of the stake, I began to thank the children and the soldiers for having allowed me to repay my debt and I asked for their forgiveness. I began to FORGIVE my inquisitors. I melted the entire scene in a big white light. In the channeled message (below) you can read the strange manner in which the past is connected to my present. My Soul had failed to forgive my inquisitors in that life and so had wanted to do it in this life. In order to do this I have been allowed me to regress to the past life involved, to that time in my personal history. When it happened the first time I thought it was because I had to understand that my role in this life was "laying on hands". In actual fact, that is only partially true, because although I do have to close that cycle by laying hands-on for healing, it also happened to allow my Soul to do what it had failed to do before: forgive.

In the message there are references to my life as a married person, you must bear in mind that I had wanted Edward exactly as he is, so that he could love me just as he loves me, long before he appeared in my life. Before knowing about the book "The Secret" I had practically materialized him exactly as I had wanted him (or so I thought). Then I had to accept the version of Edward who believes that his first wife, Sandra, who had died seven years before we met, had had her part in it too. During the first times we were together we both smelt incense, very strongly. Maybe Edward needs me for some aspects of his spiritual growth and perhaps to also bring some sort of "order" (at this moment I cannot recall a more appropriate word) in his earthly and material life.

Following is the message received during meditation/channeling by Elisa just before I started my treatment:

May 7, 2010

"Carmen cannot understand why she finds himself in the same situation as a long time ago. Now, with the knowledge that she has acquired she is able to read everything from a different point of view. Her problem is that she is unable to feel free, she is not able to tell her partner her needs without feeling guilty. Her Soul has ended up in this vicious circle once again **because she needs to learn to say no** . Her Soul needs to feel free in order to carry out her earthly duties. *(surely reiki)*

For as long as she was in the pleasure phase all was well, but now that the novelty is over the relationship problems are the same as always.

She is not far from the solution, but first her heart has to be able to forgive those who had held (*effect of other past lives dragged into this life?*) and hold her prisoner (*in the known two past lives?*). **This ancient thought form** is still affecting and influencing this life, and brings her to living situations from which she then wishes to run (*absolutely unconscious, therefore my cough ? ! ?*).

Freedom is a pure feeling, it must not be polluted by anger and resentment (*totally unconscious, I have no resentment nor anger towards anyone in this life, obviously I still have not solved the two past lives!*), so her work will initially be to find the power of forgiveness, and then after this, she will make the jump forward. She does not need anything else for the moment. In her heart she knows that this is true and all this will allow her to break away from a past that she must now learn to leave behind.

She must practice again meditation which will help her to be centered and regenerated.

In peace."

Over the past ten years I have often been told that I have "the heart chakra blocked". I gave various reasons for this, all in relation to the time that I was living at that moment, such as my divorce. More recently, exactly in January, during the treatment of an osteopath (by a family member, David) I am told for the umpteenth time that I have "a burden on my heart, a blockage of the heart chakra," which caused an outflow of tears as soon as he touched my bones and, as usual, I looked for a reason in my life right now that could have caused that "phenomenon". I had thought that that block was due to the fact that my second grandson had speech problems.

Never would I have put it in relation to my past lives.

ESSEN THERAPY JUNE 16, 2010

I already knew that during this therapy I would have had to face my past life in Venice. Elisa in turn, probably received more information to this regard, which however she did not disclose to me. She just asked me if I was ready and if I wanted to deal with that topic. As I undressed she asked me who my husband was in that life, and I replied that I had no idea, in the previous therapies done ten years before, I had never been able to see his face properly. I lay down and closed my eyes as usual. After a few minutes I found myself in the Venice of the '700 and Elisa asked me what I saw, what was going on. I experienced once again all the excitement of the first time, the fear, the anguish, the terror when I realized what my husband was about to do, etc. As I went along I described to Elisa what was happening to me. At one point, Elisa asked me to look very carefully at my husband of that time, my executioner, and to tell her who he was. I started to shake my head, it was not true, what I saw could not be, it was an invention of my mind. Again Elisa asked me to tell her who he was. I still shook my head, I did not believe what I saw, I believed that it was my mind that had put him there. I could not pronounce a word. However hard I tried to wipe the page to a blank and no matter how hard I tried to erase that image, it was still there, more and more clear. At the insistence of Elisa I replied, without being convinced. I referred that my husband at that time was Edward! I went on to describe the Mason that began to put one brick onto the other, and then Elisa asked me to ask the woman inside the wall, to ask my Soul why she had wanted to make that experience. I began to see a bright golden yellow cornfield, and a woman who was forcing two children to get into a giant cone shaped hay stack, that was at the edge of the field. The woman was frightened and scared, she had to hurry, the men were coming to get her, maybe they wanted to kill her, she was afraid they would kill the children too. With the large field fork she pushed the two children well into the haystack. The men came and took her away, dragging her because she tried to resist. The children were safe for the moment, but were in there for goodness knows how long. They eventually suffocated to death because they were never able to get out of there, the weight of the tons of hay was too much.

Elisa made me ask the two children for their forgiveness. She made me say out loud that I forgave my tormentor, my husband. In the end he was sitting by himself in a chair with the wall that was my tomb completely closed. Crying, alone and desperate for what he had done, for he had lost his beloved. In actual fact he had been the tool that had allowed me to pay my karmic debt in relation to the experience with those children.

When Elisa brought me back I was in a strong emotional state, on the one hand I did not accept on a rational level that my husband of today was the Venetian Edward, on the other hand I felt a strange sense of peace due to the understanding / experience of the karmic "cause and effect" which we are always talking about. I finally had an explanation for the irrational jealousy that I felt towards Edward during the first year of our relationship, or rather a possessive jealousy towards anything that might in the least way distract him from me. Jealousy was something that I had never in my life felt until I had met Edward. Almost as if I had to experiment and find out for myself what he had gone through In the seventeenth century when for that same feeling I had been walled alive.

———⁓⌇⌇⌇⌇⌇⌇⌇⌇⌇———

I thought I had attracted Edward to me, I thought I had wanted him, I had materialized him exactly as I wanted him, so he could love me exactly as he does. But instead, it was my Soul that was conducting me for her specific purposes, which made me enroll in the Club for singles, which attracted her former beloved and executioner in order to close that ancient cycle. It's true that when we think we've finally understood everything, we have understood nothing, or very little.

None of this has happened to "cure" or "heal" my cough but instead for fourteen long years my Soul had tried to make me understand that I had to take a path to enable myself to close the old cycles, and especially to what my Soul had not been able to forgive in those lives. My Soul had decided to complete those two paths by experiencing forgiveness in this life, and the cough was only to show me the way. The cough was to give me an indication to realize that not having found anything in the official and normal way, that is, not having found anything with the X-ray, allergy testing, special blood tests, specialist visits, etc., I had to look elsewhere, in the so-called "alternative" methods. Which after the first four years I had begun to do, but only after ten more years, that is to say only after fourteen years in total from the beginning of the cough, was I able to finally understand, to finally put all the pieces together!

If I had not met Reiki none of this would have happened. We know that for everyone, without exception, when they encounter Reiki, a door opens to "other, or to something else", and everyone has their own personal "something else".

I had thought that it was I who had to help Edward in his career and in his spiritual evolution and instead it was him who, as an unconscious instrument, allowed my Soul to evolve, to close those cycles that were still outstanding, by forgiving. He, although totally unaware, allowed me to make my important evolutionary step. Unbelievable but true.

Now my cough has improved immensely, I no longer have those violent attacks that often caused me to not even breathe, when I thought I would suffocate. Of course I still cough a little, but very rarely, and probably this will stop in September, when I will make my last Essen therapy. I know I will have to face and forgive my mother of that far century. This is the last piece missing, but the bulk of the work I have finally been able to do, thanks to our qualified Humanistic Reiki Master's course. Thanks to our teacher who made me promise to finish the course, even taking all the time I needed. In fact, I presented my little thesis more than a year after my classmates, but I kept my word, and above all, I kept the commitment I had made with myself to get to the bottom of and solve the problem of my cough, after fourteen long years.

Thank you, thank you, and thank you again to my Humanistic Reiki Master and my fellow students of the Master's course.

OTHER EXPERIENCES

To complete the picture, it seems only right to add to the above all the other "special and particular" experiences occurred to me, even if in some ways of minor importance and impact, but which are to me, still very extraordinary.

THE VIBRATIONS OF PRAYERS

In those years I had an alter in my bedroom, a tradition in many Eastern countries as was also a tradition here in Europe a couple of centuries ago. I still have today a "kamizà" (or sacred corner) in several rooms of my house. I used to sit on a "zafu" (round cushion for Zen meditation, filled with kapok) and prayed, reciting the Rosary as well as the Mala of 108 beads. I used to usually recite a rosary and then ten, twenty, thirty times or more the Mala depending on what I wanted to experience. That was the time when I was experimenting various spiritual paths so sometimes I cited a mala with a Hindu mantra, (such as Gayatri, Ohm Sai Ram, or Ohm Namaha Shivaya) and some other times with the Dalai Lama's mantra of peace, or the mantra of Tara. I did this every night unfailingly. One evening as I approached the altar to blow out the candle (before practicing I always lit a candle and some incense), that night the flame rose to at least forty centimeters. I was amazed and I froze where I was for a moment, unsure of what to do. Here again I do not feel able to give you any "technical" explanation so to speak, I can only share what I witnessed. Was it a way to express approval for the practice? Was it a way to show the presence of an Entity? Who knows? I was imbued with a pleasant feeling that is difficult for me to describe. I thanked whoever was there and went to bed comforted, knowing that I was not alone.

A year later my eldest daughter married and two of my three cousins from Luton (UK) came to Italy for the wedding. They were both daughters of my dear and beloved Aunt Aurora, who had died many years before, six months after the birth of her third child (who was one of the two coming to the wedding). My cousins were in the habit of going to a psychic to communicate with my aunt. This person, for a long period, every time they went for her advice, continued to tell them "you have a relative who prays every night in front of an altar." They were very surprised but promised to investigate with their/our relatives to try to figure out who this person might be. It turned out that none of the relatives, not even those few who had remained in Southern Italy, like our Uncle Carmine, knew anyone, not even a distant relative, who was a priest or belonged to a religious order. However, the psychic continued to insist and she repeated the same thing every time she received my cousins. No matter how hard they tried they could not find or figure out who it could be, priest, nun or other, directly related or not with them, that every night prayed in front of an altar, and which the psychic saw very clearly.

Let's return to the day of the wedding. My cousins arrived in Italy and I was really happy to host them in my villa in Graffignana for their short stay. While I was showing them the house, we got to the master bedroom and I showed them were I had a Kamizà corner made up of various masters, for example Buddha, a Madonna etc.

and that every night I sat in front of this altar to recite my prayers. "I cannot believe this, we have finally figured out who is praying every night before an altar" they exclaimed in unison. They referred to me what the English psychic had been telling them for so long. I found it amazing that my prayers were somehow captured, or "viewed" at 1500 miles away. It would seem true that our thoughts and our words create vibrations that are released in the Universe, even more so our prayers. What is that mysterious force that prayers are able to move in the Universe, so strong that a psychic can, perhaps through the family blood connection, see my acts, my praying, from so far away?

THE MYSTERY OF THE SENEGALESE BROACH

I lost my gold Senegalese pin for more than a year. I had bought it in Dakar several years earlier and always brought it with me to the various conventions . It was a baobab tree, handmade in a wax cast, therefore a unique piece. With much sorrow I discovered, that time I had wanted to wear a suit, that maybe it had been stolen in a hotel during some convention, or maybe I had forgotten it pinned to a jacket sent to the dry cleaner, (although rather unlikely). Two days before leaving for a holiday in Senegal for a month, organized with my American friend John Fay, in order to better structure my project to plant 400 fruit trees (almost all mango because they had a very long life and gave fruit for just as long) for the Mbeuguel village. This project would have yielded enough money by selling fruit to feed the entire village and would have left over enough money to send the young people of the village to school and to the University of Dakar. While preparing the luggage two days before departure, I suddenly found the brooch. It was in a small leather pouch. Now this pouch, had only one oval pocket without any other compartment inside. My daughter had used it for a trip and she had returned it to me just the previous week. It was therefore impossible that it had been there while she had used it and it certainly was not there when she returned it to me. I for sure had not put the brooch there, I hadn't seen my brooch for over a year. The pouch had been used too recently for it to be able to have been an oversight, plus the broach was too large to have been missed. The question arises now: how could my broach mysteriously reappear there all of a sudden, after such a long time?

I was leaving for Senegal with some anxiety because I was afraid of having to spend more than I could really afford. those were moments of some economic hardships for me. In Senegal there was a lot to do and I did not know exactly how much I would spend for the car hire or how much it would have cost me for the four hundred fruit trees. I had received a donation from my very good friend Tommaso C. for my tree project and my friend John had added his generous donation therefore I really had a moral obligation to carry out the project at "all costs". Was the discovery of the brooch a form of encouragement? I regarded it as a gesture to demonstrate once again that we are not alone. I was once more filled with a sense of gratitude because then, at that very moment, I knew that I would be able to plant my trees and that the project would go well.

While we were in Senegal I wanted to go to see the Animist Witchdoctor who lived in the village of Yayeme and whom I visited every time I went to Senegal. He was a great friend of the then Minister of Public Health and it was a real privilege to know him. He had also exceptionally agreed to teach me his Animist knowledge and secrets, if I were ever to stay long enough with him. This deviation from the project, as it were, allowed us two unique experiences. The first was that as we approached the village, there was still thirty kilometers to go, I started to cry for no apparent reason. At first I thought it was due to a sense of nostalgia for what had been my first experiences in that country many years before. I thought that my tears were due to the fact that I missed my friendship with a wonderful Senegalese man, a friendship that was now over. Eventually we arrived at the village with the wonder of John because the village was like an oasis in the middle of a desert. All around there was the burnt Savannah with its soil made up more of sand than earth and then all of a sudden we saw these majestic trees of mango and eucalyptus which made a pleasant shade for the entire village. We had to ask where the house of Cheickh the witchdoctor was and when we finally arrived we found only his family, his older children and his wife, Cheikh had died the year before. That's why I was crying during the journey. The family welcomed me warmly as always and I was deeply sorry for the loss of that friend and the loss of his valuable Animist knowledge, which was no longer available for me. What a terrible barrier our mind is, so much so that even when the Soul breaks through with our emotions our mind is not capable of reading its meaning. It is unable to comprehend, it is unable to receive the message that our Soul is trying to give us.

The second surprise was the fact that almost every family in the village of Yayeme were named Faye, exactly like my friend John. That was really an incredible "coincidence" and John was very moved and impressed. Since nothing happens by chance, this fact must have a meaning, even though neither of us could immediately understand exactly what this strong indication was trying to tell us. However, as a consequence, sooner or later I expect a call from John's sister or his Testamentary Lawyers because, when his time comes (hopefully not for a very long time yet) John asked me, and I accepted, to scatter his ashes in the village of Yayeme in Senegal .

Going back to the baobab broach, it reappeared the second time at a really bad time for me. I used to take with me the Senegalese broach very often on my business trips (I organized my Company's participation to the Nephrology Conventions worldwide). A few years later the broach was gone again. This time I was sure I had been careless, I was convinced that I had lost it forever. More than three years went by and I was convinced that I would never see my broach again.

In 2004 I sold my house in Graffignana (a little village in the province of Lodi, in Italy), after having been there for twenty three years and having lived the last six or seven years alone. My children had both left home, my husband had left a few years earlier, after our divorce. My son in law convinced me that it did not make much sense for me to remain in such a big house, all by myself. I therefore sold my house and went to live on the ground floor of the villa of my son in law. That afternoon in July I was really demoralized and depressed. I spent the afternoon gathering the last things in my bedroom, before the actual move which was to take place soon after. That house, which I had designed personally together with the architect, I had seen grow from nothing and become what was to have been my home for a lifetime. I thought I would leave that house only horizontally, after having seen my grandchildren and maybe even great grandchildren grow there also. As I was putting in a box all the music cassettes, one by one from the shelves where they were stacked, I took the cassette of Ajad's Reiki music of the dolphin and as I put it in the box I heard a very strange noise, as if it was empty inside and there was something else instead of a music tape, making a clinking sound. I then took it from the box where I had just placed it to see what was inside. I could not believe my eyes as my heart was filled with joy. That was really incredible. It seemed impossible, but I picked up the broach that I had not seen for so long and I burst into a joyful laughter. I spontaneously thought: " thank you, thank you and thank you once again for your presence near to me. If you wanted to surprise me to let me know that you are here, that I am not alone, you have succeeded perfectly."

I could never have put my gold broach in the music cassette, not even if I had gone crazy or if had been drunk. It was a truly strong event and a very loud and clear message. Feeling at that point light and happy, I finished emptying my bedroom, knowing I was doing the right thing for me, even though very difficult and painful. I thought I would be there forever, in that house where I had put so much of my own effort and ideas, instead it was time for me to evolve. That "death", that letting go, that lesson of "non-attachment" was a fundamental part of my evolutionary step forward.

RECENT EXPERIENCES

I had married for the second time recently and my husband invited his friends that were called "the snooker group", three of his friends he that he had known for several years and with whom he played snooker once or twice a week, and their wives. I was naturally a bit nervous with regards to the test that was waiting for me. We had renovated the whole house, which my husband had wanted to do for some time after the death of his first wife. There were therefore, many changes and novelties that evening for the old group of friends. While I was setting the table, I opened the top door of the new cabinet and prepared the crystal glasses to put on the table by placing them on a tray. When the tray was full I turned around (my back to the new furniture and facing the table) and that's when a glass fell to the ground and broke in many pieces, making a loud noise. It wasn't one of the glasses on my tray and it was not a glass from the crystal set that I had just taken, it was instead a ceramic little glass for Sakè, the typical Japanese liquor, that I had bought in Tokyo during a business trip. Among other things, there were five pieces because in Japan all sets are of five and not six like in the West. I had put them away in the back of the cabinet because I used them rarely and when I turned to see what had broken I was astonished and in disbelief. I was far away from the cabinet, I had not touched those glasses at all because they were at the bottom end of the cabinet. How did the glass from the far end of the cabinet get to the edge and then fall on the floor? It wasn't as if it was already near the edge. It was in fact very far away from the edge. My thought was

128

"ok this is a clear message, let's see what happens during the evening and I will understand if this wants to be an encouragement or a" hey you're on my territory". By the time I had finished organizing the dinner with all my typical attention to all details like flower petals on the table and arranging all the candles that I love so much, I forgot the episode entirely.

The evening passed away without any hitch of any kind, not only that, but it was a very pleasant evening. My husband's friends turned out to be really nice and they seemed to accept me with great courtesy and affability, absolutely not in a forced manner, but very natural. The dinner was a great success and so at the end of the evening I had no doubt of the significance of that glass breaking. Even though it was a somewhat strong message; for some people it could even have been a somewhat "scary" message, for me it was very positive. Along with the unequivocally strong smell of incense occurred during the first meetings with my second husband, I also considered this incident as a kind of "approval" of the entities to the path we had undertaken together.

A few years later came Richard, called "Richard the Lion Heart", the second grandson "acquired" with my second marriage. When he was about a year and a half, it happened that he lost his teddy bear, while he and his older brother Matthew were with us for the afternoon. This teddy was not only his favorite, but it was the one that accompanied him everywhere, whether to bed or to kindergarten. The incident was seen as a great tragedy by the mother of the child, the acquired daughter. She did not sleep that night and there was an exchange of phone calls and messages with my second husband, frequent and of quite an angry tone . The next day was Friday and I had to pick up my nephew Alessandro from school at Corbetta and take him to the Don Gnocchi, in Milan, for his usual speech therapy. While I was in the bathroom getting ready to go out, I brushed my hair and with (what seemed at that moment) an impetuous brush stroke on my ear, brushed off my earring and it fell in the drawer. I had left open the drawer under the sink, which was filled with various articles and cosmetics and the earring ended up amongst all that stuff. I called myself clumsy and I was very irritated because I certainly would not be able to easily find the so called "butterfly" or clip that goes behind the ear lob and holds the earring. They were rather large earrings of gold and amber, belonging to the first wife of my husband. One of the few jewels that I had kept, I had distributed all the other jewelry among my husband's two children. I would have to put another pair of earrings on because that day I just did not have the time to look for the earring (even though quite easy to find), let alone the butterfly clip that had fallen in the midst of all those bottles and toiletries. I finished brushing my hair into a pony tail and before closing the drawer under the sink, I looked for and found the earring which, as I mentioned before, was pretty big. I do not know exactly why, however, I turned the earring and to my great surprise I saw that the butterfly clip was attached to the back of the earring. I laughed with joy, with that joy that always overwhelms me when an Entity makes its presence so clear. I laughed, and loudly talking to myself I said, "I would really like some scientist to come and explain this". At that moment I realized that I had not felt any pain, like I should have done if I had taken off the earring with a brush stroke. I have pierced ears and the earrings were in the hole in my ears and clipped at the back with the butterfly, there was no way I could have brushed it off without feeling pain. I had felt instead a gentle wind on my face and neck, but I had not paid proper attention because my mind had already given a rational explanation. The butterfly still attached made me laugh too, how could it still be there? How could such a thing happen? I never talk to myself out loud, but this time I could not help but say, "Okay don't worry, I do have patience, there is no problem." I left the house and took the ring road to go and collect my nephew with the now familiar awareness that we are never alone but this time I still had in me a sense of awe at the audacity of giving me such a strong message. Who could give me a rational explanation to what had just happened, a technical or scientific version? Without removing the butterfly clip you cannot remove the earring, therefore what had really happened? In my deepest self, my Soul knew, and I could only say "thank you" again and again. In any case, the next morning the bear was found in a street near our house, near the kiosk where we had stopped to buy a comic for Matthew.

CHAPTER 7

The following is what happened immediately before I met Prof. Corbucci. In July of 2013 I fell ill, I would say seriously because it was a very violent form, and I was diagnosed with a "labyrinthitis". I was told by several doctors that the cervical arthritis problems and labyrinthitis have the same symptoms, and as I did not have other symptoms of cervical arthritis, it had to be labyrinthitis. This diagnosis was confirmed by two other ENT doctors after "maneuvering" and verifying that my iris was in fact "spinning". Technical issues and semantics aside, I was very very ill. For three days and three nights I could not stop vomiting, I could not hold down even water, and the doctor who examined me at Le Grazie, (a seaside village near Porto Venere in Italy) decided that I had to be hospitalized if prescribed medications did not work within a few hours. I went through all this with constant violent head spins that did not pass even when laying down. The three drugs (cortisone injections, suppositories and tablets) had a quick effect with regards to vomiting, but for two / three days every time I laid down and closed my eyes I had (for the first time in my life) hallucinations. I could see everything clearly with my eyes closed (even at night) and I was traveling in strange geometric shapes, which came towards me and then disappeared behind me.

The vomiting disappeared almost immediately and the strong head spins a couple of days later, but the most shocking thing for me was the weakness that followed. Probably also caused by the strong medications, the weakness did not allow me even to sit, let alone stand up, not even for just a few minutes I have never had any health problems in my life, so much so that it was my good health that enabled me to sustain a challenging job where I had to travel worldwide. From Tokyo and Nagasaki to Bangkok and Phuket, to San Francisco, New York, San Diego and New Orleans long before the tsunami, to Stockholm, Madrid and other Capitals in Europe that I am not listing here. Sometimes accompanied by colleagues, but most often alone, in addition to going up and down Italy by car, you can understand how that physical state was shocking to me.

Tokyo 1996. Outside a ceramic factory and a view of a down town shopping street only for locals, there were no tourists. I met with my Japanese colleagues the next day. I had traveled alone when going to Japan and Thailand. My Senegalese broach can be seen pinned on my jacket .

Together with my Japanese colleagues I visited several dialysis centers in Tokyo to identify those that could accommodate holiday patients.

Bangkok and Pukhet 1996 to see if there was a chance to open dialysis centers for holiday patients. I went alone and met with local colleagues.

Perhaps you can understand how, after so many years activity and travel, that terrible physical weakness was for me a real shock. How could I explain to my daughter who claimed that I was not to stay in bed too much (because the bed weakens!) that I didn't have the strength to even sit due to my profound weakness and head spins?

Whenever I had to go to the bathroom I was in danger of passing out, and only my strong will allowed me to overcome the deep malaise and not to end up on the floor every time. If I did not know deep down inside that I have to stay here a long time yet because I have a very specific task which involves many people, and if it were not for the great love I have for my children and my grandchildren, at that moment I thought it would have been much easier to slip into another life, the other life, rather than continue in that way.

As soon as it was possible we went back home to Monza, where it was cool compared to the heat wave of the seaside that year. At home we had air conditioning which had never been so much appreciated. I visited a third doctor who prescribed me two homeopathic products and advised to continue with the tablets for at least another two weeks and then until the symptoms stopped. I was still suffering from both the head spins and the general weakness. So much was the desire to get out of that nightmare that I began immediately some small and normal activities of daily life, even if I had to continuously sit down for short breaks. Unfortunately, every little "stress" made me slip back into the nightmare, do the cooking, clean the kitchen, take a shower (again with the help of my husband) were followed by head spins and the terrible feeling of weakness. Likewise, if I read or played cards, and also when I walked into a supermarket, I felt ill. The nightmare seemed to never end.

To get used to a "normal" life, in the morning we went to the Park in Monza, unfortunately, I had great difficulty there also. At first I seemed to be well, then that terrible feeling of faintness which began in the stomach and then went to the head, overwhelmed me almost blinding me. Only my strong will allowed me to get to the car without ending up on the floor, I would not give in to that feeling of faintness.

In those moments I thought that that must be how a zombie must feel, a person neither here nor there.

With every passing day, tranquility, rest, meditation and homeopathic products and especially the constant encouragement and help of my husband, I started to slowly get better. All this for as long as after three weeks from the first terrible three days. In fact, the first indication of the problem coming I had it Bibbona, in Tuscany, four or five days before those terrible three, when I had stood on the beach and I had terrible bouts of violent vomiting and dizziness for an entire day. The matter was resolved with the two injections prescribed by the doctor for medical emergencies, and the next day I was well, or so I had thought. After three weeks following the terrible three days, I was not yet independent. I was not at all well yet and it was a small consolation to be told that it would take from three weeks to a month to heal completely, and that in any case the problem could recur.

We left for our alternative vacation (we had organized a trip to Thailand that was canceled after the horrific famous three days) in Levico Terme, Trentino, putting behind us the heat and the noise of the summer. Gradually, dizziness and discomfort decreased, although I was not completely healed. In all this I tried to keep my husband calm, who in turn tried to reassure our children.

In late August, on our return home I stopped taking the medication for dizziness and soon also the homeopathic products. The disturbances reappeared mildly and occasionally, until they disappeard completely. I made another visit to another ENT specialist in Monza, who confirmed the diagnosis, saying that at Monza that spring there were several cases of "Labyrinthitis". All that remained was that slight malaise (which to be honest I also had before that experience) to remind me every now and then what I had been through, but no more dizziness. The doctor suggested that I (once again) keep the tablets always handy as dizziness could recur.

The winter passed without the return of labyrinthitis, on the other hand, though much worse around November was my walking and my knees. Every other Tuesday night we had Reiki exchange evenings and now my students knew that my knees were weak and therefore, even without my asking, during those evenings treated my knees extensively. This allowed me to sleep well at night and to be a little better for a few days. I took an x-ray and then went for a visit to an orthopedic doctor in Monza who said that I needed to have surgery. I had to have a total knee replacement, but as long as I could stand the pain I could get by with the infiltration of hyaluronic acid. The relief did not last long however and my body started, without my realizing it, to compensate with a poor posture. Slowly my knee bent, probably to avoid the full burden of my weight. I did not realize it, but my walk was more and more incorrect and, without meaning to, I created more and more damage to everything around my knee as well.

In the meantime I was trying to "take better care of myself" as suggested by a homeopathic doctor, seeking "natural" ways to improve my overall health, which resulted in a number of herbal supplements with various purposes, from the reinforcement of the intestine, strengthening the cartilage of the knee, now all used up, the homeopathic drops for coughs, a natural diuretic, a natural product prescribed by an angiologist I had been taking for three or four years, to the natural product (isoflavones) prescribed by the gynecologist more than 15 years before.

One day, after four or five months, I began feeling a sharp pain which got stronger as the days went by and I walked on it. I did Reiki every night to be able to sleep, but during the day, at every step, my pain returned. I went back to the orthopedic doctor to have another injection in my left knee and he told me that I had to decide to have surgery because it was inevitable now. Among other things, the injection was of no help, and I was in more and more pain. The following Friday, as usual, I took my nephew to the Don Gnocchi for his speech therapy, and, despite the great pain (even though I had done reiki before departure and during the journey I had kept, when possible, a hand on my knee) I was able to drive from Monza to Corbetta (near Milan) to pick him up at school and take him to Milan. Without Reiki I would probably not have been able to drive at all. The real problem came when, at the end of his therapy, as we left Don Gnocchi I absolutely could not walk, I was in terrible pain as soon as I tried putting my weight on my left leg. I was forced to stop after each step and wait for the pain to pass the acute phase before taking the next step. I was tempted to ask for a wheelchair and some help to get me to the car. That solution seemed excessive and I didn't want to frighten my nephew with all the uproar that that would have created. Then I stopped and gave myself a "distance Reiki treatment" by putting my entire figure in the bubble and visualizing my hands on my knees.

So once again I used my willpower and Reiki to get from the second floor of the Don Gnocchi to my car. When my grandson asked me why I stopped for so long at every step I explained that I had simply hurt my knee. When we finally managed to get home, I thought that it was over and forgotten for him. Instead, on the following Monday morning during the prayer session at the beginning of the day at his school, Alexander wrote, "I pray that my grandmother Carmen's knee can heal". To my daughter I simply mentioned that my knee had hurt and that I had struggled a bit to get to the car. I did not want to burden her with my problems. In actual fact I had never had such a sharp pain and I wondered to myself if I were irreparably damaging the bones of my left leg, perhaps for lack of cartilage. It was our son in law David, who is an osteopath, that comforted me and explained properly what the problem was. When I called him in despair because Reiki only worked for short periods and the orthopedic injections did not work at all, he came round to give me a session. David examined me carefully and made me "feel" for myself as well as show me, that where it hurt exactly, there were tendons, I simply had a strong tendonitis. To my bones I had done no harm whatsoever. Having never had tendinitis in my life I was not able to recognize it, but surely the orthopedic surgeon who I had visited a few days before should have been able to tell the difference! It was thanks to David's advice that gradually and finally the pain stopped: Reiki, ice and exercises to stretch the tendon worked a treat. There was also an improvement in walking but never lasted more than a few minutes, then I had to stop to allow the leg to rest and in doing so did not feel the pain so badly anymore. My walking, however, became difficult and slow.

We got to Easter, in April, when we all went to the seaside in Tuscany where my husband has a house. Two days later I found myself with the symptoms of labyrinthitis, dizziness and malaise, a feeling of faintness and a strong pain in my knees. It is to be said that "the sea throws out" all inflammations that one may have in progress. I do not know if it is true, however, it is certain that I had to take a tablet (my prescribed drug) a day for as long as I was there. Regarding the pain in my knees I did not know what to do, in addition to Reiki, which I did every morning and every evening. It was very hard for me to walk, every five or six steps I had to stop and rest my left leg, I dread to think how much more it would have hurt me without Reiki. In going up the stairs, instead, I felt a terrible pain in both legs, when going up and down the stairs. I felt pain in the tendons, the stiffened calf muscles, the general "muscles" (which I had very little of apparently) of my legs, and above all it felt and looked like my veins were about to burst. Unfortunately I have inherited from my maternal grandfather very bad blood circulation and at the age of twenty five I had had the saphenous vein in my right leg literally taken out. Of course if there had been then Prof. Corbucci's device the operation would not have been necessary. During the last visit to the angiologist I was prescribed a natural supplement to take for always. I had concerns about my veins as well, my legs were swollen and painful, especially in the summer.

Therefore, my form of defense was to use the stairs as little as possible until the situation did not improve.

As soon as we returned to Monza I went to another orthopedist for a diagnosis in relation to the new situation and to try and figure out if surgery really was the only solution. This Doctor also confirmed the general diagnosis and told me to try for a few months with a bit of physiotherapy first and if that didn't work, there was no other way. I expressed my concern about a commitment that we had taken with our grandson, which was to take him to London for five days. I needed to walk with as little pain as possible so I could do everything we had programmed. I was beginning to accept the idea that surgery was the only solution.

The painkiller along with the Reiki worked for me in London and I was able to do everything with minimal disruption of our program and the pain in my knee was bearable even though I walked with great difficulty.

I arrived in these conditions to Prof. Corbucci. in Vetralla, (Viterbo). I went directly from our seaside home and I was trying to eliminate the tablet taking one pill a day instead of two. The doctors had advised me not to stop the treatment abruptly but to take one tablet only for a few days and then stop. The second day of our stay at Vetralla we went to visit the nearby Tuscania and I almost immediately began to feel ill, practically as soon as I got in the car. I began to feel that ugly sense of fainting. I had no nausea, I simply felt faint. Once in Tuscania I had to immediately look for a pharmacy. I sat in the cool of the shop and the Doctor measured my blood pressure which was normal, but I still felt faint. I became almost a pale green, (as always when I felt that way). My husband then went out to find a bar and came back with a coffee and a pastry. I drank the coffee but unfortunately I was still unwell. Then the owner of the pharmacy came to see me, and I explained that I had not taken my tablet that morning, I had forgotten. He told me that if I really wanted the vertiserc he would give me one, but that, in his opinion, it was far more important for me to lie down in order to allow the blood to flow better towards my head. He very kindly walked me to the car (together with my husband) and they made me lie down. In fact, after five minutes or less I started to feel better and I seemed to come back to life. I was again able to give myself Reiki, I thanked the pharmacist, as I finally regained my normal color.

That afternoon I had the second session with Prof. Corbucci, and told him what had happened. He made me stand up and he corrected my posture. With my back straight, with one hand he pulled my head back. I felt a very sharp pain. He told me that I had only a strong cervical inflammation even though I had answered "no" to that question when compiling the history form before the first session.

He checked on the internet the molecule that vertiserc was composed of and told me that he could not treat me in the neck area that afternoon. The drug was a "calming" one that would not have allowed my neurological system to respond properly to his instrument. So we stayed an extra night and Prof. Corbucci the next day checked the column between the shoulder blades (rear Fourth Chakra) for my cough, and just below the attachment of the skull, at the very beginning of the spine, for my cervical problem (rear Fifth Chakra).

It was more than ten years that I suffered from that slight (and I use the word slight only because it was always temporary) and mysterious malaise that was the sense of feeling faint. No one, no doctor had ever been able to tell me what was wrong. After the classic questions like: do you suffer from diabetes, hypertension, cervical arthritis, they always ended with the conclusion that it was probably a simple problem of low blood sugar. This malaise actually coincided with the fact that I resigned from work to care for my wonderful grandson, full time. Which I actually agreed to do willingly and joyfully. Despite this, the downside was that in fact I left a job that I liked and that allowed me to travel frequently, I was in a privileged position with a Boss with whom I had a great relationship based on trust. I was responsible for a service created by myself and I had a very good assistant and collaborator. The holidays or days of permissions (which I always recuperated) were granted without problems and I approved the vacation plan for my co-worker and then my boss would approve the general plan. I found it more difficult, from one day to the next, to be able to organize my life. For whatever I wanted to do (before I could have a long interval to run some errands and then recuperate in the evening, for example) during the hours ranging from eight o'clock a.m. to eighteen hours I had to first ask my daughter. In order to replace me for a half-day, she had to ask her boss for an afternoon off, and then let me know if it was possible. This meant that for a day of "vacation" which before I obtained with a simple email to my Boss, I now had to negotiate with my daughter. She in turn had to ask and negotiate with her Boss and had to wait for a response at least until the next day, and then let me know. Maybe in my subconscious mind, I was pretty much relegated and tied down..

Anyway back to the neck and cervical arthritis and to strike a blow in favor of the medical profession it must be said that the type of problem I had with cervical arthritis was indeed rare. That is, while in the ninety-nine percent of cases the arthritis inflammation is manifested from the neck *downwards*, with a block of the neck, pain behind the head, nausea, and vomiting in some cases. My arthritis remained stuck there, maybe trying to rise to the top of the head and could not, therefore it just stuck there locked. Not giving any signs, no one could "identify it". It procured instead that sense of faintness, for lack of blood flow to the head. That is why, now I understand, that instinctively when blood is not flowing to my head, I want to lie down. After I had been lying down ten, fifteen minutes I felt good, but I had never connected it to the lack of blood to my head. So I had never been able to understand why.

You also need to know that before I complain for any health problems, I have to be *very* ill. It is very difficult to verbalize a disorder which is not considered "serious" as that uneasiness, that I seemed to be able to manage on my own, and which after a while passed anyway. So every time I sat down and drank something to push through that discomfort, sometimes mild sometimes strong, it was interpreted by the family as "laziness", and who could blame them? How could I explain to them something that I did not understand myself? Not to mention that I did not want to burden them with my problems, that I could solve alone. How could I explain to my husband that every time I laid down during the day, I then felt better? It was easier to just let them believe I was a bit lazy. Likewise with regards to our children's opinion.

Prof. Corbucci has freed me of a severe cervical arthritis, strong and subtle at the same time, which was hidden, and which exploded violently upwards, instead of downwards, as it usually happens. Exploding in those three terrible days (plus the two previous ones) involving on its way up even the inner ear with the consequences described above, with all the symptoms of labyrinthitis, when instead it was a cervica arthritis. Besides healing my legs and knees, in itself shocking, even more so was it for me to get rid of that problem, that inflammation hidden for so many years which affected me life. I finally feel good, I feel like I did ten years ago. Now I can stand in a row, no matter how long, without feeling ill after a few minutes. I can again do a lot of movements without feeling dizzy. How could I have known that I had a cervical arthritis, that instead of manifesting with the most well-known symptoms of nausea, head spins, stiff neck, stiffness in the back, it remained hidden and prevented my blood flowing to my head properly, making me every time almost faint.

How could I explain to my husband, and even more so to our children that sudden indisposition which, thankfully, then passed? Even for doctors, in fact, it was difficult to identify the two points to the right and to the left of the first neck vertebra, attached to the skull, let alone associate the discomfort that I expressed. Only the great mind of Prof. Corbucci was able to do this. Thank you Prof. Corbucci, for all you have done for me. I am grateful to my karma for this meeting which allowed me to experience this important part of my journey.

BIBLIOGRAPHY

Calligaris G., "The Wonders of Metapsychic" Publisher F.lli Bocca Editori Milan

Miranda Shaw "Passionate Enlightenment", Princeton University Press

Massimo Corbucci, "The Physics of Chance" Publisher Libri del Casato

Demetrio Iero "Modern Science and the New Heretics" Sugarco Edizioni

Holger Kerten, "Jesus Lived in India" Element Editor

Ajad, "Reiki Umanaistico" Editor Priuli & Verlucca

ACKNOWLEDGEMENTS

I sincerely thank Prof. Massimo Corbucci for allowing me to discover a new world and for having scientifically confirmed what, deep down, I already knew.

I heartily thank my sister in law Marika (Maria del Carmen Martinez Espinar, Madrilena and Castilian, Prakriti and Komyo Karuna Reiki Master, Crystal Therapist, Aroma Therapist, Doreen Virtue and Tarot Reader, creator of wonderful healing New Age jewels, who also practices Ayurvedic **Shirochampi** massage, diagnosis and treatment of the Aura and Tibetan bells treatments) who first sent me the Archangels for five days, from where it all started.

I heartily thank my sister Rosa, (Artistic painter and Amazon) who suggested the order of the chapters and wrote a forword, making the book more interesting.

Prof. Corbucci's site : www.curadelginocchio.it
Carmen D'Alessio's email: carmendalessio1948@gmail.com